THE PEOPLE OF
CORK
1600 -1799

David Dobson

CLEARFIELD

Printed for Clearfield Company by
Genealogical Publishing Company
Baltimore, Maryland
2017

ISBN 978-0-8063-5846-8

INTRODUCTION

Cork lies on the south-west coast of Ireland and is one of the biggest cities on the island. The name Cork is derived from the Irish Gaelic word signifying 'marsh'. During the 7th century it was established as a monastic settlement and later a Viking trading port. During the medieval period, from 1185, it was a stronghold of the English settlers. In the 17th century, Cork experienced an influx of Huguenots, religious refugees from France. During the Rising of 1641 and the subsequent Civil War, Cork supported the king and opposed Parliament. The city was successfully defended against the forces of Oliver Cromwell; however during the Williamite Revolution, 1688-1691, the army of William of Orange took the city in 1690. Cork lies in the Province of Munster. From the 17th century onwards, the port of Cork had significant trading links with America and the West Indies and became a major port used by emigrants. During the wars of the 18th century, many convoys assembled at the port of Cork before crossing the Atlantic.

The motto of the city, *statio fida carinis*, "a trustworthy anchorage for ships," explains why Cork became the principal harbor of the region and was of supreme importance for trade and emigration. Cork was an important link with the colonies in America and the Caribbean, with Bristol and other British ports, as well as major Continental ports.

This book has been researched and compiled from a range of primary sources, mainly in Ireland but also in England, Scotland, the Netherlands and the United States. While it does not claim to be comprehensive, the book does identify many of the inhabitants of the city of Cork during the 17th and 18th centuries and often leads to documents which should facilitate the research undertaken by historians and genealogists interested in the people of Cork.

David Dobson
Dundee, Scotland

THE PEOPLE OF CORK, 1600-1799

REFERENCES

AC	=	Annals of Cork
AcsPCCol		Acts of the Privy Council, Colonial
BM	=	British Museum
C	=	Census of Ireland
CBC	=	Council Book of the Corporation of Cork
CCCA	=	Cork City and County Archives
CPRI	=	Calendar of Patent Rolls, Ireland
CSPDom		Calendar of State Papers, Domestic
CSPI	=	Calendar of State Papers, Ireland
CTB	=	Calendar of Treasury Books
DCA	=	Dundee City Archives
DRD	=	Dublin Register of Deeds
FDJ	=	Faulkner's Dublin Journal
FHC	=	Flyn's Hibernian Chronicle
FLJ	=	Finn's Leinster Journal
GAR	=	Rotterdam Archives
HMC	=	Historical Manuscripts Commission
LRO	=	Liverpool Record Office
MAUG	=	Matriculation Album, University of Glasgow

THE PEOPLE OF CORK, 1600-1799

NARA =	National Archives & Records Administration
NRAS =	National Register of Archives, Scotland
NRS =	National Records of Scotland
NWI =	New World Immigrants
PCC =	Prerogative Court of Canterbury
PRONI =	Public Record Office of Northern Ireland
PWI =	Index to the Prerogative Wills of Ireland
SCGaz =	South Carolina Gazette
SM =	Scots Magazine
SPAWI =	State Papers, America and the West Indies
SPIre =	Calendar of State Papers, Ireland
TCD =	Trinity College, Dublin
TNA =	The National Archives, Kew
VaGaz =	Virginia Gazette
WHM =	Walker's Hibernian Magazine

THE PEOPLE OF CORK, 1600-1799

ABBOTT, ABRAHAM, a gentleman who was admitted as a Freeman of Cork in 1781. [CCCA.U11]

ABBOTT, WILLIAM, a merchant who was admitted as a Freeman of Cork in 1782. [CCCA.U11]

ABELL, ABRAHAM, a merchant in Cork, will, 1778. [PWI]

ABELL, JAMES, a merchant who was admitted as a Freeman of Cork in 1773. [CCCA.U11]

ABELL, JOHN, who was admitted as a Freeman of Cork in 1777. [CCCA.U11]

ABELL, JOSEPH, a merchant, who was admitted as a Freeman of Cork in 1740. [CCCA.U11]

ABELL, RICHARD, a merchant in Cork, will, 1802. [PWI]

ACALLEY, ELEANORE, spouse of Robert Acalley of Killhumeny, in the parish of St Finbarr's, barony of Cork, deposition, 1641. [TCD.822.193]

ACTESON, ARTHUR, a cooper who was admitted as a Freeman of Cork in 1772. [CCCA.U11]

ACTESON, ARTHUR, a cooper who was admitted as a Freeman of Cork in 1772. [CCCA.U11]

ADAMS, BENJAMIN, in Christchurch, Cork, in 1659. [C]

ADAMS, FRANCIS, a wigmaker, who was admitted as a Freeman of Cork in 1730. [CCCA.U11]

ADAMS, FRANCIS, jr., a victualler, who was admitted as a Freeman of Cork in 1790. [CCCA.U11]

THE PEOPLE OF CORK, 1600-1799

ADAMS, FRANCIS, a butcher, who was admitted as a Freeman of Cork in 1775. [CCCA.U11]

ADAMS, JONATHAN, a chandler, who was admitted as a Freeman of Cork in 1748. [CCCA.U11]

ADAMS, RICHARD, in Cork, will, 1789. [PWI]

ADAMS, ROGER, a merchant who was admitted as a Freeman of Cork in 1777. [CCCA.U11]

ADAMS, ST LEGER, a merchant, who was admitted as a Freeman of Cork in 1788. [CCCA.U11]

ADAMS, SAMUEL, in Cork, will, 1791. [PWI]

ADAMS, WILLIAM ROBERT, a merchant who was admitted as a Freeman of Cork in 1790. [CCCA.U11]

ADDIS, FENTON, a barrister, who was admitted as a Freeman of Cork in 1760. [CCCA.U11]

ADDIS, JOHN, a gentleman who was admitted as a Freeman of Cork in 1725. [CCCA.U11]

AHERN, Captain, and Miss Riorden, were married in Cork during October 1770. [FLJ.85]

AICKEN, GEORGE, a watchmaker who was admitted as a Freeman of Cork in 1778. [CCCA.U11]

AIREY, RICHARD, a gentleman who was admitted as a Freeman of Cork in 1739. [CCCA.U11]

ALDSWORTH, CHRISTOPHER, who was admitted as a Freeman of Cork in 1792. [CCCA.U11]

ALDSWORTH, RICHARD, of Anne Grove, who was admitted as a Freeman of Cork in 1784. [CCCA.U11]

ALEXANDER, ALEXANDER, who was admitted as a Freeman of Cork in 1796. [CCCA.U11]

ALEXANDER, WILLIAM, a shoemaker, who was admitted as a Freeman of Cork in 1788. [CCCA.U11]

ALLEN, ABRAHAM, a gentleman who was admitted as a Freeman of Cork in 1781. [CCCA.U11]

ALLEN, AYLMER, a brewer, who was admitted as a Freeman of Cork in 1779. [CCCA.U11]

ALLEN, AYLMER, a brewer, who was admitted as a Freeman of Cork in 1795. [CCCA.U11]

ALLEN, CHRISTOPHER, a brewer, who was admitted as a Freeman of Cork in 1765. [CCCA.U11]; married Miss Purcell in Cork in November 1770. [FLJ.90]

ALLEN, CHRISTOPHER, a gentleman, who was admitted as a Freeman of Cork in 1799. [CCCA.U11]

ALLEN, EDWARD, a gentleman, who was admitted as a Freeman of Cork in 1788. [CCCA.U11]

ALLEN, EDWARD, jr., a shipwright, who was admitted as a Freeman of Cork in 1791. [CCCA.U11]

ALLEN, GEORGE, a merchant, who was admitted as a Freeman of Cork in 1770. [CCCA.U11]

ALLEN, HENRY, a brewer, who was admitted as a Freeman of Cork in 1706. [CCCA.U11]

ALLEN, JAMES, a gentleman, who was admitted as a Freeman of Cork in 1761. [CCCA.U11]

ALLEN, JOHN, who was admitted as a Freeman of Cork in 1735. [CCCA.U11]

ALLEN, JOHN, a gentleman, who was admitted as a Freeman of Cork in 1758. [CCCA.U11]

ALLEN, JOHN, a clothier, who was admitted as a Freeman of Cork in 1739. [CCCA.U11]

ALLEN, JOSHUA, who was admitted as a Freeman of Cork in 1722. [CCCA.U11]

ALLEN, PHILIP, a gentleman, who was admitted as a Freeman of Cork in 1777. [CCCA.U11]; Mayor of Cork in 1800. [CBC]

ALLEN, RICHARD, who was admitted as a Freeman of Cork in 1729. [CCCA.U11]

ALLEN, RICHARD, who was admitted as a Freeman of Cork in 1787 [CCCA.U11]

ALLEN, RICHARD, jr., a clothier, who was admitted as a Freeman of Cork in 1752. [CCCA.U11]

ALLEN, SAMUEL, a merchant, who was admitted as a Freeman of Cork in 1797. [CCCA.U11]

ALLEN, THOMAS, a merchant, who was admitted as a Freeman of Cork in 1755. [CCCA.U11]

ALLEN, WILLIAM, a chandler, who was admitted as a Freeman of Cork in 1752. [CCCA.U11]

ALLEN, WILLIAM, and Mary Stafford, both Quakers, were married in Cork during September 1770. [FLJ.75]

ALLEN, WILLIAM, a brewer, who was admitted as a Freeman of Cork in 1784. [CCCA.U11]

ALLENET, JOHN, a tanner, who was admitted as a Freeman of Cork in 1761. [CCCA.U11]

ALLENET, MOSES, who was admitted as a Freeman of Cork in 1735. [CCCA.U11]

ALLIN, EDWARD, a shipwright, who was admitted as a Freeman of Cork in 1784. [CCCA.U11]

ALLIN, ELIZABETH, a widow in Cork, will, 1767. [PWI]

ALLIN, FRANCIS, a clothier, who was admitted as a Freeman of Cork in 1751. [CCCA.U11]

ALLIN, JOHN, a clothier in Cork, will, 1761. [PWI]

ALLIN, RICHARD, who was admitted as a Freeman of Cork in 1715 [CCCA.U11]

ALLIN, WILLIAM, a ship carpenter, who was admitted as a Freeman of Cork in 1784. [CCCA.U11]

ALLNET, Mr, died in Mallow Lane, Cork, in 1763. [FDJ.3814]

ALLWELL, SAMUEL, a stay-maker, and Joanna Vaughan, were married in Cork in December 1766. [FDJ.4136]

ANDERSON, JOHN, a merchant, who was admitted as a Freeman of Cork in 1787. [CCCA.U11]

ANDERSON, JOHN, from Cork, married .... Sempill, daughter

THE PEOPLE OF CORK, 1600-1799

of James Sempill MD, in Waterford in 1791. [SM.53.466]

ANDERSON and Company, merchants in Cork, 1801. [NRS.CS17.1.20/77]

ANDREWS, THOMAS, a merchant, who was admitted as a Freeman of Cork in 1770. [CCCA.U11]

ANDREWS, WILLIAM, constable of the Staple of Cork in 1699. [AC]

ANDREWS, WILLIAM, Mayor of Cork in 1705. [TNA.SP34.8.97]

ANSTANCE, JOHN, a butcher, who was admitted as a Freeman of Cork in 1752. [CCCA.U11]

ARCHDEACON, HENRY, from Cork, was admitted as a citizen of Rotterdam, Zealand, on 7 December 1752. [GAR]

ARCHER, Reverend FORESTER, who was admitted as a Freeman of Cork in 1794. [CCCA.U11]

ARCHER, JOHN, a merchant, who was admitted as a Freeman of Cork in 1787. [CCCA.U11]

ARCHER, THOMAS, a cooper, who was admitted as a Freeman of Cork in 1781. [CCCA.U11]

ARCHER, THORNHILL, a merchant, who was admitted as a Freeman of Cork in 1778. [CCCA.U11]

ARDOVIN, PETER, a merchant, who was admitted as a Freeman of Cork in 1746. [CCCA.U11]

ARDOVIN, MATHURIN, a gentleman, who was admitted as a

Freeman of Cork in 1730. [CCCA.U11]

ARDUIN, Mr, a merchant, died in Cork in 1766. [FDJ.4066]

ARMSTEAD, FRANCIS, who was admitted as a Freeman of Cork in 1772. [CCCA.U11]

ARMSTEAD, JANE, a spinster in Cork, will, 1785. [PWI]

ARMSTEAD, JOHN, a merchant, who was admitted as a Freeman of Cork in 1727. [CCCA.U11]; a merchant in Cork, will, 1771. [PWI]

ARMSTEAD, SARAH, a widow in Cork, will, 1783. [PWI]

ARMSTEAD, WILLIAM, a merchant, who was admitted as a Freeman of Cork in 1746. [CCCA.U11]

ARMSTRONG, EDMUND, of Ennis, Clare, who was admitted as a Freeman of Cork in 1776. [CCCA.U11]

ARMSTRONG, GEORGE, a merchant, who was admitted as a Freeman of Cork in 1740. [CCCA.U11]

ARMSTRONG, ROBERT, who was admitted as a Freeman of Cork in 1728. [CCCA.U11]

ARMSTRONG, ROBERT, a cooper, who was admitted as a Freeman of Cork in 1784. [CCCA.U11]

ARMSTRONG, ROBERT, who was admitted as a Freeman of Cork in 1797. [CCCA.U11]

ARTWRIGHT, HENRY, collector at the port of Cork, who was admitted as a Freeman of Cork in 1716. [CCCA.U11]

ASHE, ELIZABETH, a widow in Cork, will, 1810. [PWI]

7

ASH, JONATHAN, who was admitted as a Freeman of Cork in 1779. [CCCA.U11]

ASH, RICHARD, who was admitted as a Freeman of Cork in 1763. [CCCA.U11]

ASH, ROBERT, who was admitted as a Freeman of Cork in 1717. [CCCA.U11]

ASH, ROBERT, a gentleman, who was admitted as a Freeman of Cork in 1728. [CCCA.U11]

ASH, ROGER, who was admitted as a Freeman of Cork in 1728 [CCCA.U11]

ASHWOOD, NICHOLAS, in Cork purchased goods from the pirate Claes Campane in 1625. [AC]

ATKINS, JOHN, Mayor of Cork in 1729. [CBC]

ATKIN, Reverend JOHN THOMAS, died in Cork in January 1765. [FDJ.3936]; a cleric in Cork, will, 1765. [PWI]

ATKINS, Mrs, wife of John Atkins, a cook, died in Cork in August 1770. [FLJ.66]

ATKINS, ROBERT, Mayor of Cork in 1726. [CBC]

ATKINS, ROBERT, an alderman of Cork, died there in October 1765. [FDJ.4011]; will, 1766. [PWI]

ATKINS, ROBERT, and Miss Lavallin of Waterpark, were married at Carrigoline church, Cork in October 1770. [FLJ.88[

AUBIN, ELIAS, a French refugee in Cork, will, 1706. [PWI]

AUSTIN, ELIZABETH, a widow in Cork, will, 1762. [PWI]

AUSTEN, JANE, daughter of the late Thomas Austen a burgess of Cork, married Richard Lloyd of Rathcormack, at Christ Church, Cork, in 1763. [FDJ.3819]

AUSTEN, JOSEPH, Mayor of Cork in 1730. [CBC]

BACKSTER, GEORGE, was admitted as a Freeman of Cork in 1729. [CCCA.U11]

BAGNELL, HENRY, a merchant was admitted as a Freeman of Cork in 1786. [CCCA.U11]

BAGWELL, PHINEAS, a merchant in Cork, will, 1760. [PWI]

BAKER, ELIZABETH, a widow in Cork, will, 1792. [PWI]

BAKER, GEORGE, a merchant was admitted as a Freeman of Cork in 1782. [CCCA.U11]; a cooper in Cork, will, 1799. [PWI]

BAKER, GODFREY, a merchant was admitted as a Freeman of Cork in 1754. [CCCA.U11]; Mayor of Cork in 1769. [CBC]; will, 1788. [PWI]

BAKER, JOHN, a gentleman in Cork, will, 1795. [PWI]

BAKER, PAUL, a merchant in Cork, will, 1789. [PWI]

BAKER, PETER, a goldsmith was admitted as a Freeman of Cork in 1761. [CCCA.U11]; a gentleman in Cork, will, 1797. [PWI]

BALDWIN, ALICE, a widow in Cork, will, 1795. [PWI]

BALDWIN, HENRY, was admitted as a Freeman of Cork in 1765. [CCCA.U11]

9

BALDWIN, HUNGERFORD, a woollen draper was admitted as a Freeman of Cork in 1797. [CCCA.U11]

BALDWIN, JOHN, Mayor of Cork in 1737. [CBC]

BALDWIN, WINTHROP, a gentleman was admitted as a Freeman of Cork in 1769. [CCCA.U11]

BALL, HENRY, a gentleman was admitted as a Freeman of Cork in 1777. [CCCA.U11]

BALLARD, NORRIS, a clothier was admitted as a Freeman of Cork in 1759. [CCCA.U11]

BAND, CHRISTOPHER, in the parish of St Finbarr's, barony of Cork, deposition, 1641. [TCD. 825.188]

BANKS, ROBERT, a broker, died in Cork during November 1770. [FLJ.90]

BANKS, THOMAS, minister of Christchurch, Cork city, deposition, 1641. [TCD.823.106]

BARBER, GEORGE, a cabinet maker was admitted as a Freeman of Cork in 1773. [CCCA.U11]

BARBER, PETER, a cooper, was admitted as a Freeman of Cork in 1752. [CCCA.U11]

BARCLAY, THOMAS, married Miss Harte, daughter of Richard Harte, in Cork in 1764. [FDJ.3787]

BARNES, THOMAS, a merchant, was admitted as a Freeman of Cork in 1752. [CCCA.U11]

BARNET, EDWARD, born in Cork during 1794, buried in

Dundee, Scotland, on 11 March 1848. [DCA]

BARR, CHARLES, a skinner in Cork, will, 1743. [PWI]

BARRETT, DENIS, born in Cork during 1777, a weaver, buried in Dundee, Scotland, on 18 September 1838. [DCA]

BARRETT, EDWARD, a merchant in Cork, will, 1760. [PWI]

BARRET, J., born 1734, married Mrs Masters, born 1728, in Christchurch, Cork in 1810. [SM.72.877]

BARRETT, JOHN, in Christchurch parish, Cork, in 1659. [C]

BARRETT, RICHARD, a brewer, was admitted as a Freeman of Cork in 1774. [CCCA.U11]

BARRETT, WILLIAM, born 1616, a mariner in Cork, a witness before the High Court of the Admiralty of England in 1647. [TNA.HCA.62/26]

BARRETT, WILLIAM, born in Cork during 1773, buried in Dundee, Scotland, on 7 September 1838. [DCA]

BARRON, NICHOLAS, a priest in Cork, will, 1784. [PWI]

BARRY, DAVID, from Cork, married Ann Sprie, a widow, in the Presbyterian Church of Rotterdam, on 8 November 1702. [GAR]

BARRY, EDMUND, a Doctor of Physic in Cork, will refers to his wife Jane, children William, Edward, Nathaniel, Robert, Richard, John, Jane, and Mary; trustees alderman William Andrews, and William Masters a merchant; witnesses William Brown a merchant, Garrett Barry a clothier, and Thomas Barry a scrivener, all of Cork, Thomas Andrews, probate 13 Aril 1711. [DRD]

BARRY, EDWARD, MD, was admitted as a Freeman of Cork in 1731. [CCCA.U11]

BARRY, ELINOR, of Cork, married Mr Peterson of Kinsale, in January 1764. [FDJ.3828]

BARRY, GARRET, a woollen draper in Cork, will, 1799. [PWI]

BARRY, Reverend JOHN, was admitted as a Freeman of Cork in 1790. [CCCA.U11]

BARRY, ROBERT, a merchant in Jamaica, later in Cork, will, 1733. [PWI]

BARRY, WILLIAM, a merchant, was admitted as a Freeman of Cork in 1776. [CCCA.U11]

BARRY, Mrs, died in Cork in August 1765. [FDJ.3999]

BARTER, BENJAMIN, a cooper, was admitted as a Freeman of Cork in 1776. [CCCA.U11]

BARTER, JOHN LINDSAY, a cooper, was admitted as a Freeman of Cork in 1771. [CCCA.U11]

BARTER, WILLIAM, a cooper, was admitted as a Freeman of Cork in 1769. [CCCA.U11]

BASS, DANIEL, a wool card maker, was admitted as a Freeman of Cork in 1725. [CCCA.U11]

BASTABLE, EMANUEL GEORGE, a merchant, was admitted

as a Freeman of Cork in 1751. [CCCA.U11]

BASTABLE, JOHN STOCKDALE, a druggist and a Protestant, was admitted as a Freeman of Cork in 1794. [CCCA.U11]

BASTABLE, JOHN, a gentleman in Cork, will, 1808. [PWI]

BATE, THOMAS, of Grill Abbey, a merchant in Cork, will, 1641. [PWI]

BATEMAN, ELIZABETH, a widow in Cork, will, 1782. [PWI]

BATHURST, HENRY, a gentleman, Recorder of Cork and Kinsale, also HM Attorney for Munster, will, 1676. [PWI]

BATTIN, ABRAHAM, of Gurtagolane, in the parish of St Finbarr's, barony of Cork, deposition, 1641. [TCD.823.103]

BAXTER, GEORGE, a butcher, was admitted as a Freeman of Cork in 1743. [CCCA.U11]

BAXTER, GEORGE, a clerk, was admitted as a Freeman of Cork in 1775. [CCCA.U11]

BAXTER, JOHN THOMAS, a butcher, was admitted as a Freeman of Cork in 1775. [CCCA.U11]

BAYLY, ROBERT, clerk of the parish of St Finbarr's, barony of Cork, deposition, 1641. [TCD.823.109]

BAYLEY, SAMUEL, a merchant, was admitted as a Freeman of Cork in 1761. [CCCA.U11]

BAYLIE, WILLIAM, a gentleman in Cork, will, 1782. [PWI]

BEADES, EDWARD, a barber, formerly an apprentice to Garrett Nugent a barber surgeon, was admitted as a Freeman of Cork in 1730. [CCCA.U11]

BEADES, THOMAS, a cordiner, was admitted as a Freeman of Cork in 1761. [CCCA.U11]

BEALE, GEORGE, a merchant, was admitted as a Freeman of Cork in 1760. [CCCA.U11]; will, 1773. [PWI]

BEALE, JOSEPH HOARE, a merchant, was admitted as a Freeman of Cork in 1760. [CCCA.U11]

BEAMISH, WILLIAM, in Cork, will, 1772. [PWI]

BEAMISH, WILLIAM, a merchant, was admitted as a Freeman of Cork in 1790. [CCCA.U11]

BEAR, CHRISTOPHER, a butcher, was admitted as a Freeman of Cork in 1743. [CCCA.U11]

BEARE, ELIZABETH, a widow in Cork, will, 1787. [PWI]

BEARE, FRANCIS, a glazier, was admitted as a Freeman of Cork in 1777. [CCCA.U11]

BEARE, JOHN, a merchant in Cork, will, 1784. [PWI]

BEASLY, JOHN, a merchant, was admitted as a Freeman of Cork in 1780. [CCCA.U11]

BEASLY, JOSHUA, a merchant, was admitted as a Freeman of Cork in 1800. [CCCA.U11]

BEERE, HENRY, a cooper, was admitted as a Freeman of Cork in 1747. [CCCA.U11]

BEER, ROGER, tanner in Rathcooney, barony of Cork, deposition, 1641. [TCD.823.219]

BENNELL, RICHARD, clerk of the parish of St Finbarr's, barony of Cork, deposition, 1641. [TCD.823.109]

BELLEW, FRANCIS, formerly of St Kitts, British West Indies, later of Cork, will 1773. [PWI]

BELLEW, PATRICK, a merchant, was admitted as a Freeman of Cork in 1793. [CCCA.U11]

BENNET, CHARLES, a butcher, was admitted as a Freeman of Cork in 1775. [CCCA.U11]

BENNET, EDWARD, a Doctor of Physics, was admitted as a Freeman of Cork in 1731. [CCCA.U11]

BENNET, ELIZABETH, a widow in Cork, wills, 1749/1768/1788. [PWI]

BENNET, FRANCIS, a gentleman in Cork, will, 1722. [PWI]

BENNET, GEORGE, Mayor of Cork in 1724. [CBC]

BENNETT, JANE, a widow in Cork, will, 1695. [PWI]

BENNET, JOHN, a mariner, was admitted as a Freeman of Cork in 1752. [CCCA.U11]

BENNET, JOHN BARTER, an apothecary was admitted as a Freeman of Cork in 1775. [CCCA.U11]

BENNET, JOHN JAMES, MD, was admitted as a Freeman of Cork in 1787 [CCCA.U11]

BENNET, JOSEPH, a lawyer was admitted as a Freeman of Cork in 1718 [CCCA.U11]; Recorder of Cork, will, 1767. [PWI]

BENNET, MARY ANNE, a spinster in Cork, will, 1806. [PWI]

BENNET, PHILIP, an apothecary was admitted as a Freeman of Cork in 1764 [CCCA.U11]; he married Sally Delamain in Christ   Church, Cork, in October 1765, [FDJ.4017]; Mayor of Cork in 1798. [CBC]

BENNET, RICHARD, a cooper was admitted as a Freeman of Cork in 1751. [CCCA.U11]

BENNETT, SUSANNE, a widow in Cork, will, 1804. [PWI]

BENNETT, THOMAS, clerk of the parish of St Finbarr's, barony of Cork, deposition, 1641. [TCD.823.109]

BENNET, WILLIAM, Bishop of Cork was admitted as a Freeman of Cork in 1790. [CCCA.U11]

BENNET, Mrs, widow of Reverend Bennet of Carlisle, England, died in Cork in 1766. [FDJ.4057]

BENSON, JAMES, a merchant was admitted as a Freeman of Cork in 1751. [CCCA.U11]; he married Miss Vaughan, daughter of Benjamin Vaughan of Laurence Poultney Lane, Cannon Street, in August 1765. [FDJ.4002]

BENTLEY, WILLIAM, and Miss Alley, were married in Cork in November 1770. [FLJ.89]

BERRY, CHARLES, an apothecary was admitted as a Freeman of Cork in 1738. [CCCA.U11]

BERRIE, DAVID, from Cork, married Ann Sprie, a widow, in the Reformed Presbyterian Church in Rotterdam, Zealand, on 8 November 1702. [GAR]

BERRY, JOHN, in Christchurch parish, Cork, in 1659. [C]

BERRY, KINGMILL, Mayor of Cork in 1797. [CBC]

BERNARD, JOHN, a sail-cloth manufacturer was admitted as a Freeman of Cork in 1787. [CCCA.U11]

BERNARD, JULIUS, a sail-cloth manufacturer was admitted as a Freeman of Cork in 1786. [CCCA.U11]

BIGGS, JACOB, a clothier was admitted as a Freeman of Cork in 1789. [CCCA.U11]

BINGHAM, Mrs, wife of Thomas Bingham, died in Cork in 1766. [FDJ.4055]

BISHOP, EDWARD, an apothecary was admitted as a Freeman of Cork in 1778. [CCCA.U11]

BISS, JOHN, a cooper in Cork, will, 1737. [PWI]

BISSET, ELIZABETH, born in Cork during 1806, wife of David Carnegie, buried in Dundee, Scotland, on 27 February 1833. [DCA]

BLACK, JOHN, in Cork, a letter to his wife in Bordeaux, France, in 1738. [PRONI.1950.15]

BLACKBURN, JOHN, born 1780 in Cork, naturalised in New York in 1804, to settle in Georgia. [NWI.II.244]

BLAIR, PATRICK, MD was admitted as a Freeman of Cork in 1778. [CCCA.U11]

BLEASBY, WILLIAM, a chandler was admitted as a Freeman of Cork in 1791. [CCCA.U11]

BLENNERHASSET, WILLIAM, jr., of Tralee, married Miss Johnson, daughter of Nathaniel Johnson, in Cork in April 1765. [FDJ.3966]

BOISSEAU, PETER, master of the Providence of Cork 1705. [TNA.SP44.392.51]

BONWELL, JAMES, a merchant was admitted as a Freeman of Cork in 1788. [CCCA.U11]

BOURKE, WILLIAM, in Christchurch parish, Cork, in 1659. [C]

BOUSFIELD, JAMES, a merchant was admitted as a Freeman of Cork in 1752. [CCCA.U11]

BOWERMAN, FRANCIS, born 1610, a gentleman in Cork, a witness before the High Court of the Admiralty of England in 1642. [TNA.HCA.58.81]

BOWMAN, JOHN, a merchant and a Protestant stranger was admitted as a Freeman of Cork in 1797. [CCCA.U11]

BOWMAN, WILLIAM, a merchant and a Protestant stranger was admitted as a Freeman of Cork in 1797 [CCCA.U11]

BOYCE, THOMAS, a clothier was admitted as a Freeman of Cork in 1777. [CCCA.U11]

THE PEOPLE OF CORK, 1600-1799

BOYLE, BELLINGHAM, the Collector of Cork was admitted as a Freeman of Cork in 1747. [CCCA.U11]

BOYLE, EDMUND, Earl of Cork, born 1742, died 6 October 1798. [Somerset gravestone, England]

BOYLE, WILLIAM, master of the Betty of Cork in 1705. [TNA.SP44.392.67]

BOYLE, WILLIAM, a merchant in Cork, will, 1737. [PWI]

BRADSHAW, GEORGE, a cotton manufacturer was admitted as a Freeman of Cork in 1796. [CCCA.U11]

BRADSHAW, RICHARD, a merchant was admitted as a Freeman of Cork in 1735. [CCCA.U11]; Mayor of Cork in 1741. [CBC]

BRADSHAW, ROBERT, a cooper was admitted as a Freeman of Cork in 1780. [CCCA.U11]

BRANN, HENRY, master of the Ormond of Cork from Barbados via Kinsale bound for Holland in 1669. [CSPI.1669.213]

BRENNAN, THOMAS, a cooper was admitted as a Freeman of Cork in 1761. [CCCA.U11]

BRENON, Mrs GRIZELL, widow of Edward Brenon a merchant in Cork, will, 1755. [PWI]

BRETTON, BAYLEY, a watchmaker was admitted as a Freeman of Cork in 1775. [CCCA.U11]

BRETON, JOHN, a gentleman in Cork, will, 1671. [PWI]

BREYN, DIMES, from Cork, married Gretta Willems Brouwer, from Rotterdam, in Rotterdam, Zealand, on 15 March 1705. [GAR]

BRIDGES, EDWARD, from Cork, was admitted as a citizen of Rotterdam, Zealand, on 2 April 1735. [GAR]

BROCKLENBY, EDWARD, Mayor of Cork in 1723. [CBC]; a Quaker, died on Fenn's Quay, Cork, in 1766. [FDJ.4090]

BROCKLESBY, THOMAS, a clothier in Cork, will refers to his wife Mary, sons Richard and Thomas, Edward Barwicke a tanner in Cork, Samuel Watson a linen draper in Dublin; witnesses Robert Henderson a linen draper in Cork, William Prior a silk thruster in Cork, Thomas Barry a gentleman in Cork, and Simon Weldon, probate, 4 August 1714. [DRD][PWI]

BROOKS, JOHN, a butcher was admitted as a Freeman of Cork in 1783. [CCCA.U11]

BROOKS, THOMAS, a merchant and a Protestant stranger was admitted as a Freeman of Cork in 1771. [CCCA.U11]

BROSNAHAN, JOHN, a butter merchant in Cork, will, 1809. [PWI]

BROWNE, JOHN, a mariner was admitted as a Freeman of Cork in 1729. [CCCA.U11]

BROWN, JOHN, Lieutenant Colonel of the Marines, died in Cork in 1781. [SM.43.110]

BROWNE, RICHARD, born 1605, a merchant in Cork, a witness before the High Court of the Admiralty of England in

1627. [TNA.HCA.46.388]

BROWNE, Reverend ST JOHN, LL.D. was admitted as a Freeman of Cork in 1746. [CCCA.U11]

BROWN, SAMUEL, from Cork, a merchant in Nevis, British West Indies, probate 1712 PCC. [TNA]

BROWN, THOMAS, a brewer, was admitted as a Freeman of Cork in 1712. [CCCA]

BROWNE, THOMAS, a gentleman in Cork, will refers to his daughter Mary wife of Hugh Millerd jr., grandson Thomas son of Hugh Millerd, sister Sarah Humpston, grandson William Kingsmill, grandson Thomas son of Edward Browne, Evan David a clerk, witnesses William Olliffe in Cork, Theodore Rhoda a merchant in Cork, William Lane a gentleman in Cork, and Ed. Bans, probate 8 March 1717. [DRD]

BROWNE, THOMAS, Mayor of Cork in 1727. [CBC]

BROWNE, WARHAM JEMMETT, a merchant was admitted as a Freeman of Cork in 1770. [CCCA.U11]

BROWNE, WILLIAM, in the parish of St Finbarr's, barony of Cork, deposition, 1641. [TCD.823.115]

BRUNKER, Sir HENRY, Lord President of Munster, was buried in St Mary's, Cork, in 1607. [AC]

BRYAN, HENRY, of Insheggin, in the parish of St Finbarr's, barony of Cork, deposition, 1641. [TCD.824.231]

BUCK, FAITH, a widow in Cork, will, 1770. [PWI]

BUDDS, JOHN, a linen draper, died in Cork in February1765. [FDJ.3945]

BUNBERRY, JOHN, a merchant in Cork, will, 1742. [PWI]

BUNWORTH, ELIZABETH, a spinster in Cork, will, 1796. [PWI]

BURGESS, DANIEL, a cooper was admitted as a Freeman of Cork in 1795. [CCCA.U11]

BURGESS, JOHN, a cooper was admitted as a Freeman of Cork in 1778. [CCCA.U11]

BURKE, JOHN, in Queen Street, Cork, will, 1803. [PWI]

BURN, CARLETON, a woollen draper was admitted as a Freeman of Cork in 1799. [CCCA.U11]

BURNETT, THOMAS, a merchant was admitted as a Freeman of Cork in 1757. [CCCA.U11]

BURNINSTON, ANTHONY, a merchant was admitted as a Freeman of Cork in 1794. [CCCA.U11]

BURROUGHS, THOMAS, a barrister was admitted as a Freeman of Cork in 1759. [CCCA.U11]

BURROWS, HUGH, the elder, in the parish of St Finbarr's, barony of Cork, deposition, 1641. [TCD.825.186]

BURTT, RICHARD, a glazier was admitted as a Freeman of Cork in 1758. [CCCA.U11]

BURY, JOHN, in Cork, will, 1769. [PWI]

BURY, PHINEAS, a merchant was admitted as a Freeman of Cork in 1730. [CCCA.U11]; Mayor of Cork in 1759. [CBC]

BURY, THOMAS, in Cork, will, 1774. [PWI]

BUSTEED, FRANCIS, a brewer was admitted as a Freeman of Cork in 1795. [CCCA.U11]

BUSTEED, JOHN, a printer, and Sarah Saunders, were married in Cork during October 1770. [FLJ.88]

BUSTEED, MICHAEL, a merchant was admitted as a Freeman of Cork in 1773. [CCCA.U11]; Mayor of Cork in 1799. [CBC]

BUSTEAD, WILLIAM, Mayor of Cork in 1751. [CBC]; will, 1774. [PWI]

BUSTEED, Mrs, wife of Jonathan Busteed of Black Rock, died in Cork during October 1770. [FLJ.80]

BUTLER, EDMUND, born 1721 in Cork, an indentured servant in Yorktown, Virginia, absconded in 1746. [VaGaz.504]

BUTLER, HELEN, a widow in Cork, will, 1782. [PWI]

BUTLER, JOHN, in Cork, will, 1692. [PWI]

BUTTERFIELD, FRANCIS, husbandman, in the parish of St Finbarr's, barony of Cork, deposition, 1641. [TCD.825.53]

BURY, PHINEAS, Mayor of Cork in 1759. [CBC]

CAHILL, Mrs Mary, wife of Mr Cahill and widow of Captain Templeman master of the privateer <u>Anson</u>, died in Cork 1766. [FDJ.4047]

CAILLON, JOSIAS, in Cork, will, 1709. [PWI]

CALLANAN, JOHN, MD in Cork, will, 1748. [PWI]

CALLANAN, MICHAEL, an apothecary in Cork, will, 1801. [PWI]   23

THE PEOPLE OF CORK, 1600-1799

CAMPBELL, COLIN, Captain of the 24th Regiment of Foot, and Eliza Hungerford, daughter of Thomas Hungerford of the Island, were married in Cork in May 1789. [WHM.280]

CAMPBELL, COLIN, in Cork, will, 1810. [PWI]

CAMPION, ARTHUR, in Cork, will, 1793. [PWI]

CAMPION, Mrs BANE, born 1683, died in Cork in 1791. [SM.53.49]

CAMPION, Mrs, widow of Mr Campion an attorney, died in Cork in July 1770. [FLJ.57]

CAMPION, THOMAS, in Cork, will, 1761. [PWI]

CANTILLON, THOMAS, a ship-wright in Cork, will, 1810. [PWI]

CAREY, alias BOYLE, alias CARTWRIGHT, ELIZABETH, Hanover Street, Cork, will refers to her relative Thomas Cartwright of the Navy Office in London, her brother-in-law John Craggs a gentleman in Cork, Alderman George Wright, her father John Cartwright, witnesses Mathias Smith a gentleman in Cork, Catherine Berry wife of Charles Berry an apothecary in Cork, Thomas Hill a gentleman in Cork, probate 8 March 1739. [DRD]

CARLETON, FRANCIS, Mayor of Cork in 1780. [CBC]

CARLETON, Reverend ROBERT, Dean of Cork, will, 1735. [PWI]

CARR, ADAM, a mariner in Cork, will, 1794. [PWI]

CARRE, AUGUSTUS, in Cork, will, 1747. [PWI]

24

CARRUTHERS, CHRISTOPHER, sometime a manufacturer in Paisley, Scotland, now in Cork, 1801. [NRS.CS17.1.20/11]

CASEY, JOHN, a gentleman in Cork, will, 1795. [PWI]

CASEY, JOHN, a card-maker in Cork, will, 1800. [PWI]

CASEY, JOHN, in Princes Street, Cork, will, 1811. [PWI]

CAST, JOHN, master of the Diligent of Cork trading with the Leeward Islands, English West Indies, in 1669. [CSPIre.1669]

CAVENDISH, ELIZABETH, a widow in Cork, will, 1797. [PWI]

CHANDLEE, JOSEPH, a clerk in Cork, will, 1783. [PWI]

CHANEY, ROBERT, in Christchurch parish, Cork, in 1659. [C]

CHAPPELL, JOHN, gentleman, in the parish of St Finbarr's, barony of Cork, deposition, 1641. [TCD.822.168]

CHARTRES, WILLIAM, senior, in Cork, will refers to his wife Mary, his eldest son William Chartres, his grandson William Chartres Fitzwilliam, his son John Chartres, his son Thomas Chartres, Philip French and John Morley aldermen in Cork, his tenants William Allen, John Connor and William Martin; witnesses John Maurnan a pewterer in Cork, William Rose in County Limerick, and William Evans a gentleman in Cork, Robert Wallis a Notary Public in Cork, and William Simmins a gentleman in Cork, probate 31 January 1724. [DRD][PWI]

CHATTERTON, Sir JAMES, Mayor of Cork in 1767. [CBC]; will, 1806. [PWI]

CHATTERTON, THOMAS, Sub Sheriff of County Cork, and Catherine Carew of Tuckey's Quay, were married in Cork in July 1770. [FLJ.58]; will, 1794. [PWI]

CHILCUTT, Mrs, a widow, died in Cork in September 1770. [FLJ.76]

CHIP, Captain, born 1667, died in Cork in 1755. [SM.17.366]

CHUTE, RICHARD, and Mary, daughter of the late Thomas Austen, married in Cork in 1766. [FDJ.4071]

CHUTE, THOMAS, a merchant in Cork, will, 1758. [PWI]

CLARKE, CHARLES, a surveyor in West Passage, Cork, will, 1793. [PWI]

CLARKE, Mrs REBECCA, died in Cork during March 1764. [FDJ.3847]

CLARKE, WILLIAM, a burgess of Cork, will, 1774. [PWI]

CLARKE, Mrs, a widow, born 1680, died in Cork in May 1765. [FDJ.3970]

CLEMENTS, RICHARD, a merchant in Cork, will, 1692. [PWI]

COCKERILL, WILLIAM, in Cork, will, 1707. [PWI]

CODD, MARK, in Cork, will, 1789. [PWI]

COLE, JOHN, sr., a cooper in Cork, will, 1800. [PWI]

COLEY, RICHARD, a butcher, died in Cork in June 1770. [FLJ.49]

COLLINS, CORNELIUS, foreman to Alderman John Smith,'was barbarously murdered and stripped of his cloaths by some villains unknown on the road near Glasheen and dragged from thence to a field near Gill Abbey, where the corps was discovered this morning by some laborers going to work', 16 September 1765. [FDJ.4007]

COLLIS, ARTHUR, a gentleman in Cork, will, 1775. [PWI]

COLLIS, CHRISTOPHER, Mayor of Cork in 1770. [CBC]

COLTHURST, NICHOLAS, the town major of Cork in 1685. [CBC]

COLTHURST, NICHOLAS, a mariner in Cork, will, 1751. [PWI]

COMAN, Mrs ELEANOR, relict of John Coman, died in Cork during March 1764. [FDJ.3850]

COMERFORD, JOHN, a merchant in Cork, will, 1769. [PWI]

COMERFORD, PATRICK, of Cork, and Teresa Gleadowe of Dublin were married in Bath, England, in August 1770. [FLJ.66]; will, 1796. [PWI]

COMERFORD, PETER, a gentleman in Cork, will, 1800. [PWI]

CONNELL, HENRY, tobacconist, and the widow Barren, were married in Cork in September 1770. [FLJ.74]

CONNELL, TIMOTHY, married Joanna Galway in Cork in October 1765. [FDJ.4014]

CONNELL, WILLIAM, in Cork, will, 1793. [PWI]

CONNOR, JOHN, a Quaker imprisoned in Cork, around 1660. [CSPI.344.60]

CONRAN, CHRISTOPHER, sr., in Cork, will, 1772. [PWI]

CONROY, DENNIS JAMES, born 1771 in Cork, naturalised in New York in 1806. [NWI.II.245]

CONWAY, CHARLES, in Christchurch parish, Cork, in 1659. [C]

COOK, EDWARD, of Kilkenny, was appointed Searcher of Cork in 1726. [AC]

COOK, LUCRETIA, a Quaker, imprisoned in Cork, circa 1660. [CSPI.344.60]

COOK, THOMAS, a Quaker merchant in Cork, trading with the West Indies in 1686. [SPAWI.1686.910][CSPI.328.101]

COOLEY, JOHN, and Mary Anne Masterson, married in Cork in 1766. [FDJ.4078]

COOPER, WALTER, in Christchurch, Cork, in 1659. [C]

COOTE, JOHN, surveyor of Bantry, died in Cork in 1766. [FDJ.4117]

COPINGER, JAMES, and Mary his mother, 'an ancient native and inhabitant of Cork' petitioned King Charles II in 1670. [CSP.Dom.Signet Office VII, 382]

COPINGER, MICHAEL, in Cork, will, 1785. [PWI]

COPPINGER, NICHOLAS FRANCIS, in Cork, a letter, 179-. [NRS.GD21.650]; will, 1806. [PWI]

COPINGER, STEPHEN, 'an ancient native and inhabitant of Cork' petitioned King Charles II in 1670. [CSP.Dom.Signet Office VII, 382]

COPPINGER, STEPHEN, a merchant in Cork, will, 1808. [PWI]

COPINGER, THOMAS, 'an ancient native and inhabitant of Cork' petitioned King Charles II in 1670. [CSP.Dom.Signet Office VII, 382]

COPLEY, JOHN, in Cork, will, 1758. [PWI]

CORNOCKE, ISAAC, a merchant in Cork, will, 1691. [PWI]

COSSART, ELIZABETH, a widow in Cork, will, 1808. [PWI]

COTTER, Reverend GEORGE SACKVILLE, and his wife Margaret, in Cork, a marriage settlement, 1792. [PRONI.D2466.4.2]

COTTER, MAURICE, a merchant in Cork, will, 1760. [PWI]

COUGHLAN, RICHARD, a gentleman in Cork, will, 1796. [PWI]

COGLAN, ELLINOR, a spinster in Cork, will, 1798. [PWI]

COVENEY, DANIEL, a tailor in Cork, will, 1804. [PWI]

COVENEY, THOMAS, born 1762, a mariner from Cork, was naturalised in South Carolina in 1805. [NARA.M1183]

COVETT, RICHARD, in Christchurch, Cork, in 1659. [C]

COVING, THOMAS, born 1760 in Cork, emigrated to America before 1783, a citizen of South Carolina by 1795, died in St

George's parish, Colleton District, S.C., on 10 April 1815.
[SCGaz: 2.3.1815]

CRAGGS, JANE, wife of John Craggs a gentleman in Cork,
will refers to her sister Elizabeth Boyle or Cartwright; witnesses
– Elizabeth Warren a widow in Cork, Margrett Rickotts, wife of
Josias Ricketts a mariner, Charles Berry an apothecary in Cork,
and Thomas Hill a gentleman in Cork, probate 8 March 1739.
[DRD]

CRAGGS, JOHN, a gentleman in Cork, will, 1755. [PWI]

CRAGGS, LESLIE, in Cork, will, 1787. [PWI]

CRAIG, JAMES, a distiller at Hammond's marsh, Cork, will,
1806. [PWI]

CRAIG, WILLIAM, a distiller in Cork, will, 1809. [PWI]

CRAIG, WILLIAM, a gentleman in Cork, will, 1810. [PWI]

CRAMER, AMBROSE, Mayor of Cork in 1725. [CBC]

CRANE, JEREMIAH, a ship builder, died in Cork in August
1765. [FDJ.3993]

CRAVEN, JEFFORD, a gentleman in Cork, will, 1723. [PWI]

CRAWFORD, ARTHUR, eldest son of William Crawford a
merchant in Cork, matriculated at Glasgow University in 1800.
[MAUG]

CREAGH, BARTHOLEMEW, in Cork, will, 1804. [PWI]

CREAGH, DAVID, Sergeant of Cork in 1609. [AC]

CREAGH, JOHN, sr., a merchant in Cork, will, 1790. [PWI]

CREAGH, MICHAEL, a merchant in Cork, will, 1764. [PWI]

CREED, EDWARD, in Cork, will, 1806. [PWI]

CREED, REBECCA, a widow in Cork, will, 1809. [PWI]

CROFTON, ELIZABETH, a widow in Cork, will, 1786. [PWI]

CROFTS, BENJAMIN, in Christchurch, Cork, in 1659. [C]

CROFTS, CHRISTOPHER, in Cork, will, 1712. [PWI]

CROFTS, EDMOND, in Christchurch, Cork, in 1659. [C]

CROFTS, GEORGE, a cooper in Cork, will, 1760. [PWI]

CROFTS, PHILIP, a gentleman in Cork, will, 1730. [PWI]

CROKER, BRIDGET, a widow in Cork, will, 1797. [PWI]

CROKER, RICHARD, a gentleman in Cork, will, 1732. [PWI]

CROKER, SAMUEL, Mayor of Cork in 1732. [CBC]

CRONE, DANIEL, Mayor of Cork in 1748. [CBC]

CRONE, DANIEL, Alderman of Cork, died 1766. [FDJ.4037]

CRONIGAN, Mrs ANNE, sister in law to James Harnett, died in Cork during February 1764. [FDJ.3840]

CRONIN, CORNELIUS, a gentleman in Cork, will, 1802. [PWI]

CROSS, ABRAHAM, died on Nyrl's Quay, Cork, in 1804. [SM.66.479]

CROSS, EPENETUS, in Cork, will, 1704. [PWI]

CROSS, JANE, in Cork, will, 1787. [PWI]

CROSSE, SYLVESTER, a merchant in Cork, will, 1644. [PWI]

CROWLEY, HUMPHREY, a merchant in Cork, will, 1762. [PWI]

CROWLEY, HUMPHREY, Mayor of Cork in 1789. [CBC]; will, 1796. [PWI]

CROWLEY, MARGARET, a widow in Cork, will, 1767. [PWI]

CROWLEY, PATRICK, a merchant in Bandon Road, Cork, will, 1796. [PWI]

CUDMORE, MARY, a widow in Christchurch parish, Cork city, a deposition, 1641. [TCD.822.248]

CULLIMORE, DANIEL, a merchant in Cork, will, 1769. [PWI]

CUTHBERT, ELLINOR, a widow in Cork, will, 1783. [PWI]

CUTHBERT, THOMAS and JOHN, merchants in Cork, 1782. [NRS.CS17.1.1/98]

CUTHBERT, THOMAS, in Cork, will, 1756. [PWI]

DALE, WILLIAM, in Christchurch parish, Cork, in 1659. [C]

DALTERA, JAMES, a gentleman in Cork, will, 1802. [PWI]

DALY, DANIEL, master of the Gift of God of Cork was captured on its return voyage from St Martins in France by the privateer Dragon in 1649. [TNA.HCA.13.61.352]

THE PEOPLE OF CORK, 1600-1799

DALY, DANIEL, a merchant in Cork, will, 1730. [PWI]

DALY, JEREMIAH, a woollen-draper in Cork, will, 1796. [PWI]

DALY, JOHN, master of the Unity of Cork 1642. [TNA.HCA.13.58.4]

DARGIN, THOMAS, a victualler in Cork, will, 1760. [PWI]

DAVEY, Mrs, a widow, died in Cork during July 1770. [FLJ.61]

DAVID, ROCHE, from Guyenne in France, settled in Cork by 1698. [TNA.SP34.8.97]

DAVIES, Reverend ROWLAND, Dean of Cork, will, 1722. [PWI]

DAVIES, Reverend THOMAS, in Cork, will, 1795. [PWI]

DAVIS, HENRY, port surveyor of Cork, will 1799. [PWI]

DAVIS, JONAS, from Cork, emigrated via Liverpool in 1698 bound for America. [LRO]

DAWSON, ELIZABETH, wife of R. Dawson in Cork, will, 1804. [PWI]

DAWSON, GEORGE, merchant in Cork, will, 1625. [PWI]

DAY, ELLEN, a widow in Cork, will, 1798. [PWI]

DAY, RODGER, born 1805 in Cork, a private soldier of the 77th Regiment of Foot, was buried in Dundee, Scotland, on 15 January 1835. [DCA]

DAYLY, CHARLES, in Christchurch, Cork, in 1659. [C]

DEACON, JAMES, of Gurtagolan, in the parish of St Finbarr's, barony of Cork, deposition, 1641. [TCD.825.243]

DEADY, Captain, of Cork, 'several years on the West India trade', died in Dominica, British West Indies, in 1765. [FDJ.4023]

DEANE, ALEXANDER, a builder in Cork, will, 1806. [PWI]

DEANE, ROBERT, an attorney, died in Cork in November 1765. [FDJ.4022]

DEAVES, EBENEZER, a merchant in Cork, will, 1810. [PWI]

DELACOURT, ROBERT, in Cork, will, 1797. [PWI]

DELAHOID, HARMER, in Cork, will, 1793. [PWI]

DELAHOID, ROWLAND, an alderman of Cork, will, 1734. [PWI]

DELANY, EDWARD, a clerk in Cork, will, 1799. [PWI]

DENNIS, JAMES, a merchant in Cork, will, 1757. [PWI]

DENNIS, JOHN, a joiner in Cork, will, 1743. [PWI]

DENNISON, Major JOHN, a property owner in the South Liberty of Cork in 1656. [CSPIre]

DENROCHE, CHARLES, a merchant in Cork, will, 1795. [PWI]

DENROCHE, STEPHEN, a merchant in Cork, will, 1787. [PWI]

DENNY, ARTHUR, an army sergeant from Cork, who died overseas, probate 1693, PCC. [TNA]

DESPOND, DANIEL, a publican, died in Cork in 1766. [FDJ.4070]

DEVEREAUX, JOHN, MD in Cork, will, 1772. [PWI]

DEVONSHER, ELIZABETH, a spinster in Cork, will, 1757. [PWI]

DEVONSHER, JONES, a merchant in Cork, will, 1756. [PWI]

DEVONSHER, SARAH, a widow in Cork, will, 1757. [PWI]

DEVONSHER, THOMAS, a merchant in Cork, will, 1694. [PWI]

DEVONSHIRE, CHRISTOPHER, a merchant in Cork, will, 1726. [PWI]

DICKINSON, CHARLES, a brass-founder, and Abigail Austen, were married in Cork in August 1770. [FDJ]

DICKS, ELIZABETH, a widow in Cork, will, 1749. [PWI]

DICKSON, HUGH, was appointed as the Collector of Cork on 24 October 1734. [CTB.II.687]

DIGBY, JOHN, formerly of Cork, late of Surrey, England, will, 1805. [PWI]

DILLON, Mr, died on Tuckey's Quay, Cork, in 1764. [FDJ.3802]

DOBBIN, WILLIAM, a gentleman in Cork, will, 1770. [PWI]

DOHARTY, MARGARET, a widow in Cork, will, 1789. [PWI]

DONNOGHUE, JOHN, a merchant in Cork, will, 1784. [PWI]

DONOVAN, DENNIS, a sail maker, died in Cork in July 1765. [FDJ.3987]

DONOVAN, JAMES, a saddler in Cork, emigrated to Charleston, South Carolina, in 1775, a Loyalist. [TNA.AO12.52.365]

DONOVAN, MORGAN, married Meliad French, daughter of Savage French, in Cork in 1766. [FDJ.4075]; will, 1802. [PWI]

DONWORTH, ROBERT, a gentleman in Cork, will, 1747. [PWI]

DOVE, WILLIAM PRICHARD, born 1790, a ship carpenter from Cork, was naturalised in South Carolina in 1813. [NARA.M1183]

DOWMAN, JOHN, jr., a merchant, married Anne Colthurst, of Carrig, County Cork, in Cork in August 1765. [FDJ.4000]

DOWNES, ABRAHAM, died in Cork during July 1770. [FLJ.61]

DOWNES, DIVE, Bishop of Cork, will, 1709. [PWI]; his wife Elizabeth, will, 1707. [PWI]

DOWNS, Mrs, wife of Ensign Downs, and daughter of ..... Vowell, died in Cork in April 1765. [FDJ.3961]

DOWRICH, THOMAS, born 1596 in Cork, an armiger and Captain of Foot, a witness before the High Court of the Admiralty of England in 1646. [TNA.HCA.60.461]

DOYLE, Mrs, wife of Andrew Doyle a printer, died in Cork during November 1770. [FLJ.89]

DREDGE, JOHN, a gentleman in Cork, will, 1736. [PWI]

DRING, ANDREW, a merchant in Cork, will, 1759. [PWI]

DRIVER, JOHN, a saddler, 'was found murdered at his house in Pig Alley, near Shandon Church, Cork; he was mangled in a shocking manner. The Coroner's verdict was held on his body and brought their verdict – wilful murder by the wife of the deceased and other persons unknown.' [FDJ3959]

DUDLEY, HENRY, born 1785 in Cork, naturalized in New York in 1804, to settle there. [NWI.II.344]

DUNN, JOHN, a grocer from Cork, was naturalised in South Carolina in 1799. [NARA.M1183]

DUNN, Mrs, died in Blackpool, Cork, in 1764. [FDJ.3806]

DUNNAHY, JOHN, a merchant in Cork, will, 1793. [PWI]

DUNSCOMBE, GEORGE, in Cork, will, 1753. [PWI]

DYER, Mr, a glazier, died in Cork during July 1770. [FLJ.58]

DYMOND, ELIZABETH, a widow in Cork, will, 1695. [PWI]

DYMOND, PHILIP, a merchant in Cork, a persecuted Quaker, petitioned King Charles II, around 1660. [CSPIre.344.60]

EAGER, ANN, a widow, late of Cork, now in Bristol, England, will, 1800. [PWI]

EASON, ARTHUR, a tallow-chandler in Cork, will, 1769. [PWI]

EASON, PETER, jr., a merchant, was admitted as a Freeman of Cork in 1783. [CCCA]; a gentleman in Cork, will, 1802. [PWI]

EASON, Mrs, wife of Peter Eason a hardware merchant in Cork, died in 1764. [FDJ.3786]

EASON, ROBERT, jr., son of Robert Eason, a cooper, was admitted as a Freeman of Cork in 1740. [CCCA]

EASON, WILLIAM, a merchant, was admitted as a Freeman of Cork in 1748. [CCCA]

EBURNE, WILLIAM, a merchant in Cork, will, 1762. [PWI]

EDMONDS, WILLIAM, a cooper, was admitted as a Freeman of Cork in 1783. [CCCA]

EGAN, CARBERRY, in Cork, will, 1805. [PWI]

EGAN, JOHN, in Cork, will, 1807. [PWI]

EGAN, STEPHEN, a merchant, was admitted as a Freeman of Cork in 1761. [CCCA]

ELLIOT, JOSEPH, a clothier, was admitted as a Freeman of Cork in 1734. [CCCA]

ELLIOTT, MARTIN, in South Liberty of Cork, will, 1805. [PWI]

ELLIS, JAMES, a merchant, was admitted as a Freeman of Cork in 1751. [CCCA]

ELLIS, Reverend WILLIAM, Rector of Cloughnakilty, died in Cork in February 1764. [FDJ.3839]

ELMSBY, FRANCIS, a clothier in Cork, will, 1763. [PWI]

EMMET, THOMAS ADDIS, born 1763 in Cork, from Bordeaux, France, to America, naturalised in New York in 1804, to settle there. [NWI.II.244]

ENGAN, DANIEL, a merchant, was admitted as a Freeman of Cork in 1795. [CCCA]

ENOCK, JANE, a widow in Cork, probate 1694, PCC. [TNA]

EVANS, JOHN, a woollen draper, was admitted as a Freeman of Cork in 1795. [CCCA]

EVANS, ROBERT, a saddler, was admitted as a Freeman of Cork in 1783. [CCCA]

EVANS, WILLIAM, a shipwright, was admitted as a Freeman of Cork in 1752. [CCCA]

EVANSON, CHARLES, a woollen merchant, was admitted as a Freeman of Cork in 1783. [CCCA]

EVANSON, NATHANIEL, died in Cork in 1766. [FDJ.4077]

EXHAM, JOHN, a merchant, was admitted as a Freeman of Cork in 1780. [CCCA]

EYRE, EDWARD, a merchant, was admitted as a Freeman of Cork in 1730. [CCCA]

FAIR, JOHN, a cooper, was admitted as a Freeman of Cork in 1790. [CCCA]

FALKINER, CALEB, a merchant in Cork, will, 1745. [PWI]

FALKINER, MARY, a widow in Cork, will, 1766. [PWI]

FALLEN, Mr, a West India merchant, married Miss Sullivan, daughter of Mr Sullivan a bookseller, in Cork in 1766. [FDJ.4131]

FALVEY, JOHN, a barrister, was admitted as a Freeman of Cork in 1791. [CCCA]

FARMER, MARTHA, a spinster in Cork, will, 1808. [PWI]

FARMAR, ROBERT, in Cork, will, 1749. [PWI]

FARRELL, MARGARET, a widow in Cork, will, 1760. [PWI]

FARREN, THOMAS, Mayor of Cork in 1736. [CBC]

FARRINGTON, WILLIAM, of Cork, and the widow How of Bandon, were married in July 1770. [FLJ.61]

FARTHING, ELIZABETH, a spinster in Cork, will, 1751. [PWI]

FARTHING, ROBERT, in Cork, will, 1738. [PWI]

FAULKNER, Mrs, wife of Captain Faulkner commander of a vessel of Cork, died at Brickfield, Cork, in October 1765. [FDJ.4014]

FENN, EDWARD, a brewer in Cork, will, 1729. [PWI]

FENN, JOSEPH, in Cork, will, 1725. [PWI]

FENN, WILLIAM, a sugar baker in Cork, will, 1732. [PWI]

FENNELL, JOSHUA, married Miss Newsom, daughter of John Newsom a merchant in Cork, in the Quaker Meeting House in Cork in August 1765. [FDJ.3998]

FENNELL, ROBERT, a merchant in the parish of St Mary's Shandon, barony of Cork, deposition, 1641. [TCD.824.234]

FENNELL, THOMAS in Christchurch parish, Cork, in 1659. [C]

FENNELL, THOMAS, a butcher, was admitted as a Freeman of Cork in 1783. [CCCA]

FENNELL, WILLIAM, a merchant, was admitted as a Freeman of Cork in 1792. [CCCA]

FENNELL, Mrs, a seed seller, died in Cork in July 1770. [FLJ.58]

FENTON, SAMUEL, a merchant, was admitted as a Freeman of Cork in 1792. [CCCA]

FENUCAN, BRIAN, a barrister, was admitted as a Freeman of Cork in 1769. [CCCA]

FERGUSON, CHARLES, a merchant in Cork, was admitted as a Freeman of Cork in 1783. [CCCA]; died in Cork 1794. [SM.56.62]

FERGUSON, Dr ROBERT, born 1722, died in Cork 1810. [SM.72.880]

FERGUSON, ..., of Kevins-port, and the widow Taylor from Liverpool, were married in Cork during July 1770. [FLJ.61]

FERRIS, ELISHA, a gentleman in Cork, will 1786. [PWI]

FINCH, WILLIAM, a merchant, was admitted as a Freeman of Cork in 1743. [CCCA]; will, 1779. [PWI]

FISHER, BETTY, late in Youghal, a widow in Cork, will, 1810. [PWI]

FISHER, GABRIEL, a merchant, was admitted as a Freeman of Cork in 1790. [CCCA]

FISHER, JAMES, a merchant, was admitted as a Freeman of Cork in 1770. [CCCA]

FITTON, Miss DOROTHEA, died in Cork during October 1770. [FLJ.83]

FITTON, RICHARD, the elder, a tanner in Cork, will, 1758. [PWI]

FITTON, RICHARD, a brewer in Cork, will, 1760. [PWI]

FITTON, RICHARD, a merchant, was admitted as a Freeman of Cork in 1773. [CCCA]

FITTON, WALTER HUSSEY, a cooper, was admitted as a Freeman of Cork in 1787. [CCCA]

FITTON, WILLIAM, a brewer, was admitted as a Freeman of Cork in 1759. [CCCA]

FITTON, WILLIAM, a brewer, was admitted as a Freeman of Cork in 1778. [CCCA]

FITTON, WILLIAM, a burgess of Cork, will, 1786. [PWI]

FITZADAM, HARRY GOULD, in Cork in 1609. [AC]

FITZEDWARD, EDWARD GOULD, was admitted as a Freeman of Cork in 1609. [AC]

FITZEDWARD, JOHN ROCH, a native and resident of Cork in

1641, was granted freedom from quit rents on 10 October 1669. [CSPIre]; 'an ancient native and inhabitant of Cork' petitioned King Charles II in 1670. [CSP.Dom.Signet Office VII, 382[]

FITZFRANCIS, PIERS TYRRY, a juryman in Cork 1609. [CBC]

FITZGARRETT, PHILIP GOULD, a juryman in Cork in 1609. [CBC]

FITZGEORGE, STEPHEN SKYDDY, a juryman in Cork, 1609. [CBC][AC]

FITZGERALD, DAVID, a merchant in Cork, will, 1763. [PWI]

FITZGERALD, GAMALIEL, in Summerhill in the Liberty of Cork, will, 1749. [PWI]

FITZGERALD, JOHN, a native and resident of Cork in 1641, was granted freedom from quit rents on 10 October 1669. [CSPIre]; 'an ancient native and inhabitant of Cork' petitioned King Charles II in 1670. [CSP.Dom.Signet Office VII, 382[]

FITZGERALD, JOHN, a cooper, was admitted as a Freeman of Cork in 1735. [CCCA]

FITZGERALD, JOHN, a cooper, was admitted as a Freeman of Cork in 1794. [CCCA]

FITZGERALD, ROSE, a spinster in Cork, will, 1753. [PWI]

FITZGERALD, THOMAS, a barrister, was admitted as a Freeman of Cork in 1781. [CCCA]

FITZGERALD, THOMAS, of Bandon, married a daughter of Redmond Fitzgerald of Cork, in Cork, 1763. [FDJ.3817]

FITZGERALD, WILLIAM, in Cork, will, 1700. [PWI]

FITZJOHN, JAMES GALWAY, a gentleman and a juryman in Cork in 1709. [CBC]

FITZJOHN, JOHN ROCHE, at the North Gate of Cork, in 1609. [CBC]

FITZJOHN, MAURICE ROCHE, a native of Cork, petitioned King Charles II for the restoration of his houses in Cork in 1663. [CSPIre.345.188]

FITZMAURICE, MICHAEL, a livery stable keeper in Cork, will, 1799. [PWI]

FITZNICHOLAS, PHILIP GOULD, a yeoman in Cork, in 1609. [AC]

FITZPATRICK, ADAM GOULD, was admitted as a Freeman of Cork in 1609. [AC]

FITZPATRICK, JOHN ROCH, a native and resident of Cork in 1641, was granted freedom from quit rents on 10 October 1669 [CSPIre]; 'an ancient native and inhabitant of Cork' petitioned King Charles II in 1670. [CSP.Dom.Signet Office VII, 382[

FITZPHILIP, EDMUND MARTELL, a juryman in Cork, 1609. [CBC]

FITZRICHARD, JAMES MIAGH, Petty Porter of North Gate of Cork in 1609. [AC]

FITZRICHARD, JOHN ROCHE FITZMORRIS, in Cork, and his son and heir Richard John Fitzjohn, 1627. [CPRIre]

FITZRICHARD, WILLIAM TYRRY, in Cork, 1609. [CBC]

FITZSIMONS, Mr, and Nelly Morris, were married in Cork during October 1770. [FLJ.83]

FITZSTEPHEN, NICHOLAS SKIDDIE, a merchant in Cork, 1627. [CPRIre]

FITZSTEPHEN, STEPHEN, son and heir of David Terry Fitzstephen, late Alderman of Cork, 1631. [CPRIre.]

FITZWILLIAM, DOMINICK ROCHE, an Alderman of Cork in 1632. [IPR.596]

FITZWILLIAM, THOMAS GOULD, a juryman in Cork in 1609. [CBC]

FLEETWOOD, THOMAS, in Christchurch parish, Cork, 1659. [C]

FLEMING, DANIEL, from Cork, married Clementina Forbes from Dunbar, Scotland, in London in 1755. [SM.17.268]

FLEMING, NOBLETT, a glazier, was admitted as a Freeman of Cork in 1767. [CCCA]

FLEMING, THOMAS, a cooper, died in his house in Francis Street, Cork, in May 1765. [FDJ.3967]

FLEMING, WILLIAM, a merchant, was admitted as a Freeman of Cork in 1778. [CCCA]

FLETCHER, ROBERT, in Christchurch parish, Cork, in 1659. [C]

FLETCHER, ROBERT, a gentleman in Cork, will, 1686. [PWI]

FLOYDE, HENRY, in Cork, will, 1656. [PWI]

FLYNN, RUBY, a cooper, was admitted as a Freeman of Cork in 1783. [CCCA]

FOGARTY, BUTLER, a merchant, was admitted as a Freeman of Cork in 1776. [CCCA]

FOOT, JOHN, a wine merchant, was admitted as a Freeman of Cork in 1800. [CCCA]

FORD, FRANCIS, a clothier, was admitted as a Freeman of Cork in 1782. [CCCA]

FORD, HENRY, a wool comber, was admitted as a Freeman of Cork in 1782. [CCCA]

FORD, JOHN, a cooper, was admitted as a Freeman of Cork in 1791. [CCCA]

FORD, SAMUEL, a clothier, was admitted as a Freeman of Cork in 1769. [CCCA]

FOREMAN, LUKE, a merchant, was admitted as a Freeman of Cork in 1783. [CCCA]

FORREST, JASPER, born 1606 in Cork, a merchant, a witness before the High Court of the Admiralty of England in 1627. [TNA.HCA.46.366]

FOULKES. JAMES, a goldsmith, was admitted as a Freeman of Cork in 1781. [CCCA]

FOURKE, HENRY, a brewer, was admitted as a Freeman of Cork in 1796. [CCCA]

FOWKE, JOSEPH, a merchant in Cork, will, 1780. [PWI]

FOWKE, SAMUEL, in Cork, will, 1805. [PWI]

FOWKE, YELVERTON, a gentleman in Cork, will, 1783. [PWI]

FRANCE, ROSE, a widow in Cork, will, 1793. [PWI]

FRANCIS, EDWARD, a gentleman in Cork, will, 1721. [PWI]

FRANCKLAND, THOMAS, a gentleman in Cork, will, 1686. [PWI]

FRANKLAND, AGNES, a widow in Cork, will, 1787. [PWI]

FRANKLAND, BARRY, in Cork, will, 1734. [PWI]

FRANKLAND, RICHARD, MD in Cork, will, 1763. [PWI]

FRANKLIN, ANDREW, Mayor of Cork in 1761. [CBC]

FRANKLIN, DANIEL, a shoemaker, was admitted as a Freeman of Cork in 1781. [CCCA]

FRANKLIN, JOHN, a merchant, was admitted as a Freeman of Cork in 1783. [CCCA]

FRANKLIN, Sir JOHN, Mayor of Cork in 1785. [CBC]; will, 1796. [PWI]

FRANKLIN, RALPH, a surgeon in Cork, will, 1655. [PWI]

FRANKLYN, EBENEZER, a widow in Cork, will, 1744. [PWI]

FRANKS, MATTHEW, an attorney, was admitted as a Freeman of Cork in 1784. [CCCA]

FREEMAN, JANE, a widow in Cork, will, 1783. [PWI]

FREEMAN, JOHN, in the parish of St Finbarr's, barony of Cork, deposition, 1641. [TCD.822.229]

FREEMAN, WILLIAM, in Cork, a letter, 1718. [PRONI.D2707.A1.1.1.2A]

FREKE, Sir J., Mayor of Cork in 1753. [CBC]

FRENCH, ABRAHAM, a merchant, was admitted as a Freeman of Cork in 1711. [CCCA]

FRENCH, GREGORY, yeoman in parish of Rathcooney, barony of Cork, deposition, 1641. [TCD.825.69]

FRENCH, JAMES, a merchant in Cork, will, 1746. [PWI]

FRENCH, JAMES JOSEPH, a merchant, was admitted as a Freeman of Cork in 1793. [CCCA]

FRENCH, PHILIP, a merchant, was admitted as a Freeman of Cork in 1711. [CCCA]

FRENCH, RICHARD, ironmonger, in the parish of St Finbarr's, barony of Cork, deposition, 1641. [TCD.824.164]

FRENCH, SAVAGE, a merchant, was admitted as a Freeman of Cork in 1768. [CCCA]; his wife died in Bath, England, in May 1765. [FDJ.3969]; he married Miss Millerd, in Cork during October 1770. [FLJ.79]; will, 1770. [PWI]

FRENCH, THOMAS, only son of Abraham French, an Alderman, was admitted as a Freeman of Cork in 1738. [CCCA]

FRENCH, TWOGOOD, a barrister, was admitted as a Freeman of Cork in 1760. [CCCA]; will, 1770. [PWI]

FRITH, WILLIAM, a cooper, was admitted as a Freeman of Cork in 1790. [CCCA]

FRYER, SAMUEL, a silversmith, was admitted as a Freeman of Cork in 1795. [CCCA]

FULLER, ABRAHAM, a linen draper in Cork, will, 1769. [PWI]

FULLER, EDWARD, a merchant, was admitted as a Freeman of Cork in 1788. [CCCA]

FULLER, GEORGE, a merchant, was admitted as a Freeman of Cork in 1751. [CCCA]

FULLER, GEORGE, Mayor of Cork in 1734. [CBC]

FULLER, JAMES, a merchant, was admitted as a Freeman of Cork in 1776. [CCCA]

FULLER, THOMAS, jr. a merchant, was admitted as a Freeman of Cork in 1747. [CCCA]

FULLER, THOMAS, a merchant, was admitted as a Freeman of Cork in 1790. [CCCA]

FULLER, WILLIAM, Mayor of Cork in 1739. [CBC]

FULLER, WILLIAM, son of Thomas Fuller, was admitted as a Freeman of Cork in 1740. [CCCA]

FULLER, WILLIAM, a merchant, was admitted as a Freeman of Cork in 1757. [CCCA]

FULLER, Miss, an authoress, died near Cork in 1790. [SM.52.363]

FULHAM, MICHAEL JOSEPH, a merchant in Cork, will, 1808. [PWI]

FULTON, Miss, died in Cork during October 1770. [FLJ.83]

GALWAY, EDMOND, in Cork, will, 1794. [PWI]

GALWAY, FRANCIS, in Cork, will, 1802. [PWI]

GALWEY, PATRICK, a gentleman in Cork, will, 1706. [PWI]

GALWAY, JOHN, a native and resident of Cork in 1641, was granted freedom from quit rents on 10 October 1669. [CSPIre];

GALLWAY, JOHN, in Cork, will, 1712. [PWI]

GALLWAY, RICHARD, a pilot in Cork, 1609. [AC]

GALWAY, WILLIAM, in Cork, a Roman Catholic who was licensed to bear arms in 1705. [HMC.Ormonde.11.476]

GAMBLE, ELIZABETH, a widow in Cork, will, 1749. [PWI]

GAMBLE, GEORGE, in Christchurch parish, Cork, in 1659. [C]

GARESHES, JANE, late of Dublin, a widow in Cork, will, 1743. [PWI]

GARDNER, JOHN, in Christchurch parish, Cork, in 1659. [C]

GARRET, JOHN, a chocolate maker, died in Cork in July 1770. [FLJ.62]

GARRATT, JOSEPH, a chocolate maker in Cork, will, 1793. [PWI]

GARROD, HENRY, in Cork, will, 1763. [PWI]

GASH, JOHN, late Collector of Cork, 1717. [AC]

GAY, CHARLES, of Knockagen, on behalf of John Tucker of the same address, his father in law, deposition, 1641. [TCD.825.242]

GETHING, RICHARD, born 1608 in Cork, an armiger, a witness before the High Court of the Admiralty of England in 1647. [TNA.HCA.62.65]

GIBBES, DANIEL, a gentleman in Cork, will, 1724. [PWI]

GIBBONS, Reverend EBENEZER, minister of the Baptist Congregation in Cork, died there in March 1764. [FDJ.3848]

GIBBS, DANIEL, of Derry in County Cork, died in Cork in 1764. [FDJ.3812]

GILLMAN, HAYWARD, a gentleman in St Finsbarr's, Cork, will, 1732. [PWI]

GILLMAN, JOHN, the elder, of Currisure, Cork city, deposition, 1641. [TCD.825.206]

GILMAN, JOHN, the younger, in the parish of St Finbarr's, barony of Cork, deposition, 1641. [TCD.825.234]

GILLMAN, JOHN, a gentleman in Curriheen, Liberty of Cork, will, 1746. [PWI]

GILLMAN, ST LEGER HAYWARD, a gentleman in Curriheen, Liberty of Cork, will, 1758. [PWI]

GILLMAN, STEPHEN, in Curriheen, South Liberty of Cork, will, 1740. [PWI]

GLASSCOKE, WILLIAM, a gentleman in Cork, will, 1633. [PWI]   51

GLISSAN, ANDREW, a woollen draper in Moregh, Cork, will, 1794. [PWI]

GODDARD, HOLLAND, a merchant in Cork, will, 1720. [PWI]

GODDARD, JOHN, from Cork, was admitted as a citizen of Rotterdam, Zealand, on 14 June 1716. [GAR]

GODDARD, WILLIAM, a merchant in Cork, an indenture, 1699. [AC]

GODFREY, ELIZABETH, a widow in Cork, will, 1751. [PWI]

GOGGIN, Mrs, wife of Mr Goggin a merchant, died in Cork in August 1770. [FLJ.67]

GOLD, IGNATIUS, a merchant in Cork, in 1667. [CSPIre.1667]

GOLLOCK, REBECCA, a widow in Cork, will, 1811. [PWI]

GOOD, JOHN, in Cork, a lease, 1799. [PRONI.D2404.4.5]

GOOLD, FRANCIS, a merchant, died in Cork during July 1770. [FLJ.61]; will, 1771. [PWI]

GOOLD, GEORGE, a merchant in Cork, will, 1789. [PWI]

GOOLD, MARY CATHERINE, in Cork, will, 1805. [PWI]

GOOLD, THOMAS, an alderman in Cork, will, 1658. [PWI]

GORMAN, MICHAEL, a merchant in London, and Rebecca Stacpole, daughter of Philip Stacpole a merchant, were married in Cork in September 1770. [FLJ.71]

GOUGH, FRANCIS, a gentleman in Cork, will, 1695. [PWI]

GOUGH, WILLIAM, from Cork, was admitted as a citizen of Rotterdam, Zealand, on 23 April 1710. [GAR]

GOULD, HELEN, a widow in Cork, will, 1746. [PWI]

GOULD, HENRY FITZDAVID, a merchant in Cork, a will, 1714. [PWI]

GOULD, JAMES, a native and resident of Cork in 1641, petitioned King Charles II on 28 November 1664, and was granted freedom from quit rents on 10 October 1669. [CSPIre]; 'an ancient native and inhabitant of Cork' petitioned King Charles II in 1670. [CSP.Dom.Signet Office VII, 382[]

GOULD, LAURENCE, a merchant in Cork, will, 1735. [PWI]

GOULD, MICHAEL, in Cork, will, 1673. [PWI]

GOULD, MORRIS, a yeoman in Cork in 1609. [AC]

GOULD, NICHOLAS, a gentleman, a juryman in Cork in 1609. [CBC]

GOULD, PATRICK FITZEDMOND, a merchant in Cork, will, 1681. [PWI]

GOULD, ROBERT, a juryman in Cork in 1609. [CBC]

GOULD, STEVEN, a native and resident of Cork in 1641, was granted freedom from quit rents on 10 October 1669. [CSPIre]; 'an ancient native and inhabitant of Cork' petitioned King Charles II in 1670. [CSP.Dom.Signet Office VII, 382]

GRAHAM, PERCIS, a widow in Cork, will, 1787. [PWI]

GRANT, MARY, in Cork, will, 1760. [PWI]

GRANT, WILLIAM ALEXANDER, in Cork, will, 1795. [PWI]

GRAVENOR, SAMUEL, in Christchurch parish, Cork, in 1659. [C]

GRAY, FRANCIS, in Cork, will, 1799. [PWI]

GRAY, JOHN, a merchant in Cork, will, 1751. [PWI]

GRAY, JOSEPH, a merchant in Cork, will, 1774. [PWI]

GRAY, POPE, in Cork, will, 1791. [PWI]

GRAY, STEPHEN, a merchant in Cork, will, 1737. [PWI]

GREATRAKES, Mrs, mother of Counsellor Greatrakes, died near Cork in June 1770. [FLJ.51]

GREGG, THOMAS, a gentleman in Cork, will, 1811. [PWI]

GREGORY, MARY, a persecuted Quaker in Cork, who petitioned King Charles II in 1660. [CSPIre]

GREY, JAMES, was granted property in Cork in 1646. [CSPI.1657.844]

GRIFFIN, SIMON, from Cork, and Margaretha Opheys from Velno in Limburg, were married in the Scots Kirk in Rotterdam, Zealand, in 1736. [GAR]

GUBBINS, JOSEPH, a merchant in Cork, will, 1759. [PWI]

GUYNAN, MARY, a widow in Liberty of Cork, will, 1772. [PWI]

HADDOCK, Mrs, wife of Edward Haddock a cabinet maker in Cork, died in June 1770. [FLJ.49]

HALL, DORCAS, a widow, in the parish of St Finbarr's, barony of Cork, deposition, 1641. [TCD.823.110]

HALL, JOHN, a clerk, in the parish of St Finbarr's, barony of Cork, deposition, 1641. [TCD.824.224]

HALL, JUSTANCE, in the parish of St Mary's Shandon, Cork city, deposition, 1641. [TCD.82.154]

HALY, FRANCIS, in Cork, will, 1792. [PWI]

HALEY, MAURICE, father of three sons born in Cork in 1770. [SM.32.457]

HALY, JOHN, MD, married Miss Mullan, in Cork in November 1765. [FDJ.4021]

HALY, ROBERT, a native and resident of Cork in 1641, was granted freedom from quit rents on 19 October 1669. [CSPIre]; 'an ancient native and inhabitant of Cork' petitioned King Charles II in 1670. [CSP.Dom.Signet Office VII, 382[

HALY, Mrs, wife of John Haly MD, died in Cork in 1766. [FDJ.4092]

HAMAN, JOHN, senior, in Cork, will, 1692. [PWI]

HAMAN, JOHN, a merchant in Cork, will, 1718. [PWI]

HAMAN, MARY, in Cork, and Joshua Beale in Mountmellick, Queen's County, a Quaker marriage certificate, 1686. [PRONI.D2278.1A]

HAMLYN, JOHN, in Christchurch parish, Cork, in 1659. [C]

HARDING, HENRY, Mayor of Cork in 1789. [CBC]

HARDING, JOHN, Mayor of Cork in 1779. [CBC]

HARDING, PETER, born 1642, a farmer who died near Cork in 1755. [SM.17.414]

HARDING, RICHARD, in Cork, will, 1773. [PWI]

HARDING, THOMAS, a burgess of Cork, will, 1810. [PWI]

HARDING, VALENTINE, a merchant in Cork, will, 1750. [PWI]

HARDING, WILLIAM, a gentleman in Cork, will, 1714. [PWI]

HARDING, WILLIAM, Mayor of Cork in 1756. [CBC]; will, 1763. [PWI]

HARDING, Mrs, wife of Henry Harding, died in Cork in 1766. [FDJ.4126]

HARE, WILLIAM, a linen-draper in Cork, will, 1759. [PWI]

HARGRAVE, ABRAHAM, an architect in Cork, will, 1808. [PWI]

HARMAN, SAMUEL, in Cork, will, 1809. [PWI]

HARMON, THOMAS, a watchmaker, and Miss Barrett, were

married in Cork during October 1770. [FLJ.80]

HARMAN, Mrs, wife of Joshua Harman a clothier, died in Cork in December 1765. [FDJ.4030]

HARNET, DANIEL, a merchant in Cork, will, 1793. [PWI]

HARNET, JAMES, in Cork, will, 1780. [PWI]

HARPER, ISABELLA, a widow in Cork, will, 1783. [PWI]

HARRIS, JOHN, in Cork, will, 1805. [PWI]

HARRIS, JOSEPH, in Cork, will, 1723. [PWI]

HARRIS, JOSEPH, in Cork, will, 1799. [PWI]

HARRIS, RICHARD, Mayor of Cork in 1790. [CBC]; will, 1798. [PWI]

HARRIS, ROBERT, born 1606 in Cork, a gentleman aboard the Elizabeth of Youghal, a witness before the High Court of the Admiralty of England in 1627. [TNA.HCA.46.310]

HARRIS, STEPHEN, in Christchurch parish, Cork, in 1659. [C]

HARRIS, THOMAS, in Cork, will, 1803. [PWI]

HARRISON, JANE, died on Hammond's Marsh, Cork, during January 1764. [FDJ.3828]

HARRISON, JOSEPH, a gentleman in Cork, will, 1772. [PWI]

HARROLD, EDMOND, a merchant in Cork, died in Bath, England, in 1764. [FDJ.3809]

HARTFIELD, Colonel CHARLES, in Cork, a letter, 1797. [PRONI.D607.E165]

HARTIGAN, WILLIAM, a surgeon in Cork, a letter, 1798. [PRONI.D607.F.258]

HARVEY, FRANCIS, a merchant in Cork, will, 1809. [PWI]

HARWOOD, JOHN, searcher at the port of Cork in 16... [CSPT.344.3]

HASLETT, ROGER, born 1780, a paver from Cork, was naturalised in South Carolina in 1828. [NARA.M1183]

HAWKES, HENRY, of Powllymore, parish of Gallygrahane, Cork City, deposition, 1641. [TCD.822.69]

HAWKES, JOHN, a tallow-chandler in Cork, will, 1804. [PWI]

HAWKINS, ANNE, a widow in Cork, will, 1736. [PWI]

HAWKINS, JOHN, in Christchurch parish, Cork, in 1659. [C]

HAWKINS, JOHN, a merchant in Cork, will, 1707. [PWI]

HAWKINS, JOHN, a gentleman in Cork, will, 1734. [PWI]

HAYES, ATWELL, in Cork, will, 1798. [PWI]

HAYES, BENJAMIN, an attorney-at-law in Cork, will, 1803. [PWI]

HAYES, JOSEPH, a merchant in Cork, will, 1795. [PWI]

HEARD, BICKFORD, a gentleman in Cork, will, 1780. [PWI]

HEARD, WILLIAM, a gentleman in Cork, will, 1782. [PWI]

HEARNE, JOHN, a linen draper in Cork, will, 1771. [PWI]

HEGARTY, THOMAS, a gentleman in Cork, will, 1804. [PWI]

HENDERSON, ROBERT, a merchant in Cork, testament, 1741. [PWI]

HENKIER, JAMES, a merchant in Cork, will refers to his brother Patrick Henkier and his five daughters and son James, to his brother Thomas and his two sons and a daughter, to friends William Boyle, Hugh Mitchell, George Evans jr., James Morrison a merchant in Cork, witnesses William Roberts a merchant, William Chartes jr, Thomas Barry a scrivener, all of Cork, William Lane, probate 17 October 1713. [DRD]

HENNESY, BRYAN, a butter buyer in Cork, will, 1810. [PWI]

HENNESY, Mrs, wife of Maurice Hennesy master of the Lime and Salt Works in the South Mall, died in Cork in 1766. [FDJ.4055]

HERLINY, DANIEL, born 1652, a laborer, died in Cork in 1757. [SM. 49.623]

HERMAN, MARTIN, a merchant in Cork, will, 1630. [PWI]

HERRICK, ELIZABETH, a spinster in Cork, will, 1798. [PWI]

HEWITT, THOMAS, in Cork, will, 1811. [PWI]

HICHCOCK, WILLIAM, a gentleman in Cork, will, 1783. [PWI]

HICKIE, WILLIAM, a merchant in Cork, will, 1786. [PWI]

HICKSON, ROBERT, in Cork, will, 1800. [PWI]

HIGGINS, Mrs, wife of a distiller, died in Cork during September 1770. [FLJ.73]

HILANGHT. THOMAS, from Cork, and Janet Jones, ["Janntgen Jans"], from Dysart, Fife, Scotland, were married in the Reformed Church in Rotterdam, Zealand, on 21 March 1649. [GAR]

HILL, ANNE, a widow in Hollyhill, Cork, will, 1780. [PWI]

HILL, JOHN, born 1577, master of the Gift of God of Cork a witness before the High Court of the Admiralty of England in 1649. [TNA.HCA.61.351]

HILL, JOHN, of Dublin, and Mary Beare, daughter of John Beare a merchant, were married in Cork in September 1770. [FLJ.72]

HILL, LYSAGHT, in the Liberties of Cork, will, 1811. [PWI]

HILL WILLIAM, a merchant in Cork, probate 1616. [PCC]

HILLARY, JOHN, a silver-smith in Cork, will, 1785. [PWI]

HINCHINE, JOHN, a cooper, and the widow Jarvis, were married in Cork in September 1770. [FLJ.74]

HINGSTON, JOHN, a merchant in Cork, will, 1746. [PWI]

HOARE, ROBERT, in Cork, will, 1764. [PWI]

HODDER, FRANCIS, in Christchurch, Cork, in 1659. [C]

HODDER, FRANCIS, a merchant in Cork, will, 1774. [PWI]

HODDER, GEORGE, Mayor of Cork in 1754. [CBC]; will, 1771. [PWI]

THE PEOPLE OF CORK, 1600-1799

HODDER, SAMUEL, in Cork, will, 1804. [PWI]

HOLMES, PATTY, daughter of the late Alderman Holmes, died in Cork in 1766. [FDJ.4083]

HOLMES, WILLIAM, Mayor of Cork in 1749. [CBC]

HONAHAN, E., in Cork, a letter, 1718. [PRONI.D2707.A1.A.2A]

HONOHANE, MARY, in Cork, will, 1731. [PWI]

HOOD, DANIEL, a stationer and book-seller in Cork, will, 1789. [PWI]

HOPKINS, ELLINOR, a spinster in Cork, will, 1792. [PWI]

HOPKINS, STEPHEN, a merchant in Cork, will, 1777. [PWI]

HOPPER, EDWARD HART, a merchant in Cork, will, 1803. [PWI]

HORE, RUSSELL, a merchant in Cork, will, 1765. [PWI]

HOUGHTON, JOHN, Mayor of Cork in 1660. [CSPIre]

HOUGHTON, THOMAS BARCROFT, in Cork, a deed, 1797. [PRONI.D645.113]

HOVELL, HUGH, a gentleman in Cork, will, 1720. [PWI]

HOVELL, WILLIAM, an alderman of Cork, will, 1698. [PWI]

HUGHES, ANN, relict of Richard Hughes a burgess of Cork, will, 1774. [PWI]

HUGHES, JOSHUA, in Cork, a lease, 1799. [PRONI.D2404.4.5]

HUGHS, TIMOTHY, an iron-monger in Cork, will, 1795.
[PWI]

HULEAT, JAMES, Mayor of Cork in 1731. [CBC]; will, 1748.
[PWI]

HULET, THEODORUS, from Cork, died aboard HMS
Portsmouth probate 1678, PCC. [TNA]

HULL, DIONATA, a widow in Cork, a petition, 1693. [AC]

HULL, ELIZABETH, in Cork, will, 1705. [PWI]

HULL, RANDALL, a merchant in Cork, a letter, 1680.
[LRS.36.163]; will, 1685. [PWI]

HULL, WILLIAM, a merchant in Cork, will, 1658. [PWI]

HUNGERFORD, BEECHER, in Cork, will, 1787. [PWI]

HUNGERFORD, THOMAS, former apprentice of William and
Peter Thompson, was admitted as a Freeman of Cork in 1741.
[CBC]

HURLEY, THOMAS, a gentleman in Cork, will, 1780. [PWI]

HURLY, TIMOTHY, a merchant in Cork, will, 1805. [PWI]

HURLEY, Mrs, died in Cork in August 1765. [FDJ.3999]

HUTCHINSON, JONATHAN, a merchant in Cork, will, 1749.
[PWI]

HUTCHINSON, Miss, daughter of Samuel Hutchinson of
Aghadown, County Cork, died in Cork in September 1765.
[FDJ.4003]

HYNES, LUKE, in Cork, will, 1810. [PWI]

HYNES, THADIE, born 1662, died in Cork in 1767. [SM.29.103]

IRELAND, ANNA MARIA, a spinster in Cork, will, 1808. [PWI]

IRELAND, JANE, a widow in Cork, will, 1810. [PWI]

IZOD, KEVAN, in the Liberties of Cork, will, 1798. [PWI]

JACKSON, AMBROSE, Mayor of Cork in 1735. [CBC]

JACKSON, MARGARET, a widow in Cork, will, 1807. [PWI]

JAMES, JAMES FRENCH, died at his house near Cork in 1793. [SM.55.414]

JAMESON, EDWARD, Commissary of the States General of the Netherlands in Cork, a letter, 1795. [NRS.GD51.2.37.1]

JENKINS, BENJAMIN, a gentleman in Cork, will, 1684. [PWI]

JEPPIE, Mr, and Miss Cross of Cork, were married there in February 1764. [FDJ.3838]

JERMIN, JOHN, and Elizabeth Jago, were married in Cork during July 1770. [FLJ.61]

JERVOIS, SAMUEL, in Cork, will, 1787. [PWI]

JOHNS, EDWARD, clerk of the parish of St Finbarr's, barony of Cork, deposition, 1641. [TCD.823.109]

JOHNSON, ANDREW, in Cork suburbs, will, 1786. [PWI]

JOHNSON, FRANCES, a widow in Cork, will, 1786. [PWI]

JOHNSON, Mrs, relict of Mr Johnson of Flemingstown, died in Cork in July 1765. [FDJ.3986]

JOHNSTON, WILLIAM, a merchant in Cork, died there in February 1764. [FDJ.3840]

JONES, THOMAS, a shop-keeper in Cork, will, 1807. [PWI]

JOYCE, WILLIAM, from Cork, settled in Newfoundland by 1770, husband of Catherine Slattery. [FHC]

KEARNEY, EDMUND, a native and resident of Cork in 1641, was granted freedom from quit rents on 19 October 1669. [CSPIre]; 'an ancient native and inhabitant of Cork' petitioned King Charles II in 1670. [CSP.Dom.Signet Office VII, 382]

KEAYS, CHRISTOPHER, a merchant in the Liberties of Cork, will, 1811, [PWI]

KEEFE, DANIEL, a butter merchant in Cork, will, 1803. [PWI]

KEENE, STEPHEN, an inn-keeper in Cork, will, 1691. [PWI]

KEILY, EDMUND, a saddler in Cork, will, 1780. [PWI]

KELLY, CHRISTOPHER, born 1782, a mariner from Cork, was naturalised in South Carolina in 1804. [NARA.M1183]

KELLY, GEORGE, parson of the rectory of Rathcooney, and prebend of St Michael's, barony of Cork, deposition, 1641. [TCD.822.235]

KELLY, ROBERT, husbandman, in the parish of St Finbarr's, barony of Cork, deposition, 1641. [TCD.825.120]

KELLY, THOMAS, a merchant in Cork, will, 1769. [PWI]

KELLY, WILLIAM, a baker in Cork, will, 1732. [PWI]

KEMP, WILLIAM FORSTER, a grocer in Cork, will, 1796. [PWI]

KENNET, RICHARD, Mayor of Cork in 1783. [CBC]

KENNEY, CHRISTOPHER, a gentleman in the Liberties of Cork, will, 1776. [PWI]

KENT, SOBER, Mayor of Cork in 1782. [CBC]

KERR, MARY, a widow in Cork, will, 1804. [PWI]

KESTERSON, WILLIAM, a gentleman in Cork, will, 1758. [PWI]

KINASTON, CHARLES, in Christchurch parish, Cork, in 1659. [C]

KINGE, WILLIAM, a gentleman in Cork city, deposition, 1641. [TCD.825.122]

KINGSMILL, HANNAH, a widow in Cork, will, 1705. [PWI]

KINGSMILL, THOMAS, a merchant in Cork, will, 1703. [PWI]

KINGSMILL, Lieutenant Colonel WILLIAM, born 1607 in Cork, a witness before the High Court of the Admiralty of England in 1646. [TNA.HCA.60.462]

KINGTON, JAMES, Mayor of Cork in 1787. [CBC]

KIRKPATRICK, WILLIAM, a merchant in Cork, will, 1742. [PWI]

KNAPP, EDMOND, an alderman of Cork, will, 1791. [PWI]

KNAPTON, E.S., in Cork, a letter, 1771. [PRONI]

KNIGHT, ALLEN, and Catherine Martin, were married in Cork in June 1770. [FLJ.52]

KNIGHT, JOHN, a mariner in Cork, will, 1700. [PWI]

KNIGHT, WILLIAM, in the parish of St Mary's Shandon, barony of Cork, deposition, 1641. [TCD.822.253]

KNIVETON, HENRY, born 1596 in Cork, a gentleman, a witness before the High Court of the Admiralty of England in 1647. [TNA.HCA.62.11]

KNOX, WILLIAM, in Cork, will, 1809. [PWI]

LAMB, Captain, and the widow Busteed, were married in Cork in 1766. [FDJ.4039]; the relict of Captain Lamb died in Cork during October 1770. [FLJ.86]

LANDER, JONAS, born 1776 in Cork, naturalised in New York in 1804, to settle there. [NWI.II.244]

LANE, RICHARD, in Christchurch parish, Cork, in 1659. [C]

LANE, ..., the only son of Robert Lane a merchant in Cork, died in January 1764. [FDJ.3833]

LARYMORE, HUGH, a wine merchant in Cork, will, 1821. [PWI;Hawkins]

LASSERE, ELIAS, a merchant in Cork, will, 1742. [PWI]

LATHAM, JOHN, and Elizabeth Brown, daughter of Thomas Brown a burgess of Cork, and niece to the Lord Bishop of Cork, in September 1770. [FLJ.72]

LAVALLINE, JAMES, a native and resident of Cork in 1641, was granted freedom from quit rents on 19 October 1669. [CSPIre]

LAVALLEN, PATRICK, an alderman in Cork, will, 1666. [PWI]

LAVIT, JOSEPH, a merchant in Cork, will, 1728. [PWI]

LAVIT, NATHANIEL, a gentleman in Cork, will, 1770. [PWI]

LAVIT, WALTER, in Cork, will, 1758. [PWI]

LAVITE, WILLIAM, Mayor of Cork in 1745 [CBC]

LAVITT, CHRISTIANA, a spinster in Cork, will, 1779. [PWI]

LAW, FRANCIS, a clerk in Cork, will, 1808. [PWI]

LAWTON, HUGH, Mayor of Cork in 1776. [CBC]

LAWTON, JOHN, a merchant in Cork, will, 1773. [PWI]

LAWTON, RICHARD, a merchant in Cork, will, 1804. [PWI]

LAWTON, TRAYER, a merchant in Cork, will, 1763, wife Ann Lawton, children Hugh Lawton, Sarah Lawton, and Lucia Lawton, grandchildren Ann Leslie and Lawton Leslie, wits. James Aickin, Daniel MacCAarthy, Robert MacCarthy, and

James Flaherty, all of Cork. [DRD]; merchant in Cork, will, 1758. [PWI]

LEAUE, TEGO, born 1603 in Cork, an indentured servant who emigrated via Plymouth to St Kitts, English West Indies, aboard the Robert Bonaventure in 1633. [PA.53]

LEWIS, ISRAEL born in Cork, a seaman aboard HMS Venable, flagship of Admiral Adam Duncan, at the Battle of Camperdown on 11 October 1797. [TNA.Adm]

LIGHTON, WILLIAM, a Lieutenant of the Royal Tyrone Regiment, in Cork, a letter, 1798. [PRONI.D623.A.150.37]

LILL, JAMES, in Cork, will, 1791. [PWI]

LILL, MARY, a widow in Cork, will, 1793. [PWI]

LIMBIRIE, JOHN, a mariner in Cork, will, 1626. [PWI]

LINDSAY, GEORGE, in Cork, will, 1745. [PWI]

LINSCOMB, RICHARD, an inn-keeper in Cork, will, 1703. [PWI]

LITCHFIELD, JOHN, a merchant in Cork, will, 1805. [PWI]

LLOYD, RICHARD, a burgess of Cork, died at Tullagreen near Cork in September 1770. [FLJ.75]

LOMBARD, GEORGE, the younger, a merchant in Cork, will, 1749. [PWI]

LOMBARD, GEORGE, a merchant in Cork, will, 1769. [PWI]

LOMBARD, JAMES, formerly of Lombardstown, now in Cork, will, 1769. [PWI]

LOMBARD, JAMES, a merchant in Cork, will, 1783. [PWI]

LOMBARD, WILLIAM, merchant in Cork, will, 1718. [PWI]

LOMBARD, WILLIAM, a merchant in Cork, will dated 30 January 1754, proved 17 October 1754, refers to eldest daughter Margaret, and second daughter of his sister Mary, and to her sons William and Simon, to his brother George and his children Anstice, Catherine, Dominick, and James, to his late brother Dominick and sons John, Dominick, Peter and Patrick, to niece Margaret Lombard and her husband Edmond Barrett, to Ellen Gallway or Lombard, to his only sister Ellen Lombard [DRD]; will, 1754. [PWI]

LONE, WILLIAM, in parish of Inishkenny, Cork city, deposition, 1641. [TCD.824.198]

LONG, PETER, a cabinet-maker, and Miss Loohy of Mallow Lane, were married in Cork in October 1770. [FLJ.88]

LORDAN, PATRICK, born 1789 in Cork, settled in Charleston, naturalised in South Carolina in 1828. [NARA.M1183]

LOVE, ABRAHAM, a gentleman in Cork, will, 1715. [PWI]

LOVE, JOHN, was appointed Collector of Cork in 1734. [AC][CTB.II.551]

LOWE, CHARLES, in Cork, will, 1809. [PWI]

LUCAS, ELIZABETH, a widow in Cork, will, 1811. [PWI]

LUCAS, JASPER, Mayor of Cork in 1795. [CBC]; a merchant in Cork, will, 1811. [PWI]

LUCEY, MAURICE, a merchant in Cork, will, 1782. [PWI]

LUCEY, THOMAS, a merchant tailor in Cork, will, 1770. [PWI]

LUGG, SAMUEL, a merchant in Cork, will, 1724. [PWI]

LUMLEY, HENRY, a gentleman in Cork, will refers to his nephew John Key, his nephew William Raincock a merchant in Penrith, Cumberland, England, George Raincock and John Raincock merchants in London, his grand-nephew Hugh Raincock a gentleman in Cork [to take the name Lumley], and Dorothy, Margaret, and Grace daughters of said Wiliam Raincock, Captain Daniel Connor of Bandon and his wife Mary Connor, and their daughters Sarah Wade, Jane Lapp, Mary Connor, Hannah Connor, and Elizabeth Connor, and their sons William Connor, George Connor, and Daniel Connor, his servant John Williams, Ellinor Murphy; witnesses William Chartres, William Kirkpatrick a merchant, and Richard Harrison, all of Cork, probate 30 April 1729. [DRD]; will, 1730. [PWI]

LYNCH, SARAH, a widow in Cork, will, 1734. [PWI]

LYNCH, Mrs, wife of Dennis Lynch of Donagmore, died in Cork during August 1770. [FLJ.68]

LYNE, JOHN, died in Brown Street, Cork, in 1764. [FDJ.3779]

LYON, WILLIAM, Bishop of Cork, will, 1627. [PWI]

LYSAGHT, JOSEPH, in Cork, will, 1799/1801. [PWI]

LYSAGHT, WILLIAM, in Cork, will, 1798. [PWI]

MCCALL, JOHN B., born 1777 in Cork, a grocer who was naturalised in South Carolina in 1808. [NARA.M1183]

MCCARTHY, CHARLES, 'an ancient native and inhabitant of Cork' petitioned King Charles II in 1670. [CSP.Dom.Signet Office VII, 382]

MCCARTHY, CHARLES, a gentleman in South Liberty of Cork, will, 1801. [PWI]

MCCARTHY, DENIS, in Travers St., Cork, will, 1810. [PWI]

MCCARTHY, MICHAEL, a notary public in Cork, will, 1784. [PWI]

MACCARTHY, Mrs, born 1684, widow of Captain MacCarthy of Cove Street, died 1787 in Cove Street, Cork. [SM.49.570]

MCCARTHY, Mrs, wife of Charles McCarthy a merchant, died in Cork in July 1765. [FDJ.3990]

MCCARTIE, CHARLES, in Cork, will, 1758. [PWI]

MCCARTIE, CHARLES, in Cork, will, 1761. [PWI]

MCCARTY, DANIEL, of Ballynamona, died in Cork in 1766. [FDJ.4107]

MCCARTY, FRANCIS, a cutler in Cork, will, 1781. [PWI]

MCCARTY, Mrs, died in Cork in 1764. [FDJ.3811]

MCCOLL, SAMUEL, in Cork, a letter, 1799. [NRS.GD51.1.334/1]

MCDERMOTT, ELIZABETH, a widow in Cork, will, 1803.
[PWI]

MCDERMOTT, HUGH, late of Cork, died in October 1765.
[FDJ.4016]

MCDERMOTT, MICHAEL, a goldsmith in Cork, will, 1784.
[PWI]

MCDERMOTT, Mrs, wife of Michael McDermott a
silversmith, died in Cork during July 1770. [FLJ.56]

MCDONALD, JAMES, born 1633, seven foot six inches tall, a
soldier from 1685 to 1716, lately a day-laborer, died near Cork
in 1760. [SM.22.447]

MCGRATH, EDWARD, born 1776 in Cork, a carpenter in
Charleston, naturalised in South Carolina in 1802.
[NARA.M1183]

MACKAY, Captain, of the Highland Regiment, and Maria
Whiting of Queen Street, Dublin, were married in Cork during
July 1770. [FLJ.61]

MCLOUGHLAN, PHILIP, a mariner in Cork, will, 1756.
[PWI]

MCMAHON, CATHERINE, a spinster in Cork, will, 1794.
[PWI]

MCMILLAN, ALEXANDER, a merchant in Campbeltown,
Argyll, Scotland, later in Cork, a deed of factory, 23 January
1765. [NRS.RD2.198.103]

MCNEMARA, BRIDGET, a widow in Cork, will, 1749. [PWI]

MCNEMARA, THOMAS, a merchant in Cork, will, 1735. [PWI]

MADOX, ANNE, a spinster in Cork, will refers to her brother Joseph Madox, Francis Harrison a clothier in Bealgooley, grandson of Laurence Harrison a tanner in Cork deceased, Catherine and Mabel, daughters of Mabel Barber a widow in Cork, Reverend Henry Maul rector of Shandon, Cork, Richard Daunt a merchant in the parish of Christ Church; witnesses James Lamon a surgeon in Cork, Richard Dalton a cordiner in Cork, Andrew Rock a gentleman in Cork; John Bastard, Thomas Barry, Daniel Crone, and John Whiting, probate 21 November 1719. [DRD]

MADRAS, ANNE, in Cork, will, 1754. [PWI]

MADRAS, JOHN, a clerk in Cork, will, 1774. [PWI]

MAGUIRE, RICHARD, an apothecary in Cork, will, 1801. [PWI]

MAHER, Mr, a cooper, died in Cork during October 1770. [FLJ.86]

MAHONY, ANDREW, a gentleman in Cork, will, 1800. [PWI]

MAHONY, CORNELIUS LAWRENCE, in Cork, will, 1753. [PWI]

MAHONY, Reverend PATRICK, of South Chapel in Cork, died there in 1763. [FDJ.3824]

MAHONY, WILLIAM, maltster on Rocksand Quay, Cork, will, 1805. [PWI]

MAINADUCK, Mrs, born 1671, died in Cork, in May 1765. [FDJ.3967]

MAINADUE, ALCIDE BONNOIT, a refugee in Cork, will, 1726. [PWI]

MALIN, ROBERT, a Quaker imprisoned in Cork circa 1660. [CSPI.344.60]

MANDERS, JONATHAN, a merchant in Cork, will, 1786. [PWI]

MANN, ISAAC, Bishop of Cork, will, 1789. [PWI]

MANSER, GEORGE, and Mary Danigan, were married in Cork during March 1764. [FDJ.3847]

MARTIN, ALEXANDER, cordwainer in Cork, will, 1758. [PWI]

MARTIN, ELIZABETH, a widow in Cork, will, 1762. [PWI]

MARTIN, MILES, gentleman in Cork, will, 1735. [PWI]

MARTIN, THOMAS, in the parish of St Mary's Shandon, Cork city, deposition, 1641. [TCD.825.94]

MARTIN, WILLIAM, in Cork, will, 1775. [PWI]

MASSIOT, JAMES, a merchant in Cork, will, 1746. [PWI]

MASTERS, EDWARD, in Christchurch, Cork, in 1659. [C]

MATHEWS, PHILIP, alderman of Cork, will, 1677. [PWI]

MATHEW, RICHARD, born 1592 in Cork, a merchant, a witness before the High Court of the Admiralty of England in 1638. [TNA.HCA.54.282]

MAUNSELL, JOHN, merchant in Cork, will, 1752. [PWI]

MAYLOR, PAUL, cooper in Cork, will, 1742. [PWI]

MAYLOR, SAMUEL, Mayor of Cork in 1766 [CBC]

MAYNARD, WILLIAM, late Collector of Cork in 1734. [AC][CTB.II.551]

MEAD, JAMES, an attorney, died in Cork in 1766. [FDJ.4103]

MEAD, JOHN, MD in Cork, will, 1704. [PWI]

MEAD, PATRICK, apothecary in Cork, will, 1734. [PWI]

MEADE, PIERCE, born 1611 in Cork, a merchant, a witness before the High Court of the Admiralty of England in 1642. [TNA.HCA.57.454]

MEAD, WILLIAM, the Recorder of Cork in 1603. [AC]

MEAD, WILLIAM, Dean of Cork, will, 1764. [PWI]

MEAGH, JAMES, in Cork, died 1 November 1666. [CSPIre,1667]

MEAGH, JOHN FITZSTEPHEN, merchant in Cork, will, 1636. [PWI]

MEAGH, ROBERT FITZDAVID, gentleman in Cork, will, 1635. [PWI]

MEAGHER, JOHN, a wine-cooper, died in Cork in July 1770. [FLJ.58]

MEE, ISAAC, merchant in Cork, will, 1799. [PWI]

MEE, TEMPERENCE, widow in Cork, will, 1736. [PWI]

MEE, THOMAS, cordwainer in Cork, will, 1736. [PWI]

MERCER, WILLIAM, in Cork, a letter, 1777. [NRS.GD190.1.156]

MERIWETHER, Captain JOHN, in Cork, will, 1780. [PWI]

MESKELL, DAVID FITZDAVID, a merchant in Cork, will, 1681. [PWI]

MIAGH, JAMES, 'an ancient native and inhabitant of Cork' petitioned King Charles II in 1670. [CSP.Dom.Signet Office VII, 382]

MIANNAGHANE, JOHN OGE, merchant in Cork, will, 1625. [PWI]

MILLARD, HUGH, Mayor of Cork in 1728. [CBC]

MILLARD, HUGH, Mayor of Cork in 1747. [CBC]

MILLARD, HUGH, the younger, and Rebecca Carleton, daughter of Francis Carleton, were married in Cork in September 1770. [FLJ.75]

MILLIKEN, ROBERT, in Cork, will, 1789. [PWI]

MINTON, JOHN, vintner in Cork, will, 1811. [PWI]

MITCHELL, DODSWORTH, eldest son of Alexander Mitchell, was admitted as a Freeman of Cork in 1741. [CBC]; gentleman in Cork, will, 1774. [PWI]

MITCHELL, JOHN, coal factor in Cork, will, 1807. [PWI]

MITCHELL, THOMAS, a merchant in Cork, later in London, will, 1691. [PWI]

THE PEOPLE OF CORK, 1600-1799

MITCHELL, Lieutenant THOMAS, in Cork, will, 1755. [PWI]

MOORE, ANN, widow in Cork, will, 1777. [PWI]

MOORE, RICHARD, eldest son of Emanuel Moore of Maryborough, died in Cork during July 1770. [FLJ.56]

MOORE, THOMAS, jr., merchant in Cork, will, 1783. [PWI]

MOORE, THOMAS, merchant in Cork, will, 1798. [PWI]

MOORE, THOMAS, in Cork, will, 1799. [PWI]

MOORE, WILLIAM, surgeon in Cork, will, 1752. [PWI]

MORGAN, GEORGE, in Cork, will, 1801. [PWI]

MORGAN, JANE, widow in Cork, will, 1788. [PWI]

MORGAN, SYMON, in Christchurch, Cork, in 1659. [C]

MORGAN, Mrs, wife of Jonathan Morgan, died in Cork in 1764. [FDJ.3790]

MORLEY, MIRIAM, widow in Cork, will, 1741. [PWI]

MORLEY, THOMAS, late of Cork, and his son and heir John Morley in 1627. [CPRIre]

MORLEY, THOMAS, in the parish of St Mary's Shandon, Cork city, deposition, 1641. [TCD.825.179]

MORLEY, THOMAS, in Christchurch, Cork, in 1659. [C]

MOROGH, ANDREW, 'an ancient native and inhabitant of Cork' petitioned King Charles II in 1670. [CSP.Dom.Signet Office VII, 382]

MORPHY, DENIS, gentleman in Cork, will, 1808. [PWI]

MORPHY, HUGH, merchant in Cork, will, 1702. [PWI]

MORRIS, ABRAHAM, merchant in Cork, will, 1722. [PWI]

MORRIS, JOHN, maltster in Cork, will, 1769. [PWI]

MORRIS, JONAS, in Cork, will, 1736. [PWI]

MORRIS, MARY, widow in Cork, will, 1793. [PWI]

MORRIS, THEOPHILUS, merchant in Cork, will, 1715. [PWI]

MORRISON, JAMES, Mayor of Cork in 1784. [CBC]

MORRISON, MICHAEL, in Cork, will, 1803. [PWI]

MORROGH, JAMES, merchant in Cork, will, 1780. [PWI]

MORROUGH, JAMES, in Cork, will, 1805. [PWI]

MORTON, THOMAS, merchant in Cork, will, 1802. [PWI]

MORTON, WILLIAM, merchant in Cork, will, 1760. [PWI]

MOYLAN, DAVID, merchant in Cork, will, 1773. [PWI]

MOYLAN, DENNIS, merchant n Cork, will, 1773. [PWI]

MOYLAN, JOHN, merchant in Cork, will, 1799. [PWI]

MOYLAN, Mrs, widow of David Moylan a merchant, died in Cork in July 1770. [FLJ.54]

MULCAHEY, TIMOTHY, son of Edward Mulcahey in Cork, and Lamberdine Hermanse, were married in the Scots Kirk in Rotterdam, Zealand, on 10 October 1744. [GAR]

MURPHY, MAURICE, butter buyer in Cork, will, 1807. [PWI]

MURPHY, PETER, from Cork, and Machteltye Jans from Elten, Emmerich, were married in the Reformed Church in Rotterdam, Zealand, on 5 April 1695. [GAR]

MUSCHAMP, A., born 1598 in Cork, an armiger, a witness before the High Court of the Admiralty of England in 1646. [TNA.HCA.60.460]

MYAGH, DAVID FITZJAMES, in Cork, will, 1671. [PWI]

NAGLE, ELIZABETH, widow in Cork, will, 1796. [PWI]

NAPIER, JEAN MACDOWELL, wife of William Augustus Kellet a banker in Cork, and daughter of the late Colonel William Napier of Culreuch, died in Cork in 1805. [SM.67.807]

NASH, LEWELLIN, in Cork, will, 1794. [PWI]

NASON, WILLIAM, merchant in Cork, will, 1740. [PWI]

NEALE, SAMUEL, in Cork, a letter, 1763, [PRONI.D1044.44]

NEEDHAM, JOHN, born 1613 in Cork, a surgeon, a witness before the High Court of the Admiralty of England in 1644. [TNA.HCA.59.395]

NELAN, MAURICE, merchant in Cork, will, 1788. [PWI]

NETTLES, Reverend ROBERT, married Miss Drew, in Cork, 1764. [FDJ.3787]

NEVELL, THOMAS, in the parish of St Finbarr's, barony of Cork, deposition, 1641. [TCD.822.35]

NEWENHAM, GEORGE, merchant in Cork, will, 1793. [PWI]

NEWENHAM, HANNAH, in Cork, will, 1749. [PWI]

NEWENHAM, JOHN, in Cork, will, 1706. [PWI]

NEWENHAM, JOHN, clothier in Cork, will, 1735. [PWI]

NEWENHAM, RICHARD, merchant in Cork, will, 1759. [PWI]

NEWENHAM, THOMAS, in Cork, will, 1725. [PWI]

NEWENHAM, THOMAS, in Cork, will, 1766. [PWI]

NEWENHAM, WILLIAM, in Cork, will, 1736. [PWI]

NEWENHAM, Mrs, wife of Thomas Newenham of Coolmore, died 1763 in Cork. [FDJ.3827]

NEWMAN, ADAM, Mayor of Cork in 1738. [CBC]

NEWMAN, CHARLES, surgeon in Cork, will, 1799. [PWI]

NEWMAN, ELIZABETH, a widow in Cork, will, 1717. [PWI]

NEWMAN, MARY, widow in Cork, will, 1797. [PWI]

NEWMAN, RICHARD, in Cork, will, 1693. [PWI]

NEWMAN, THOMAS, Customer at the port of Cork, 16... [CSPI.344.3]

NEWSOM, GEORGE, merchant in Cork, will, 1791. [PWI]

NEWSOM, JOHN, born 1706, a Quaker, died in Cork during October 1770. [FLJ.84]; merchant in Cork, will, 1770. [PWI]

NEWSOM, JOHN, sr., in Cork, will, 1810. [PWI]

NEWSOM, SARAH, widow in Cork, will, 1785. [PWI]

NICOLSON, JOHN, gentleman in Cork, will, 1802. [PWI]

NOONE, JOHN, in Cork, sergeant to Captain Wacham St Geger's company, will, 1678. [PWI]

NORCOTT, WILLIAM, married Miss Knight of Charleville, in Cork in October 1765. [FDJ.4014]

O'BRIEN, Mrs CATHERINE, died in Brown Street, Cork, in 1766. [FDJ.4130]

O'BRIEN, DIGBY, gentleman in Cork, will, 1796. [PWI]

O'BRIAN, JAMES, Collector of Cork in 1754. [AC]

O'BRIAN, JAMES, 'the famous Irish giant', died in Cork in 1804. [SM.66.647]

O'BRIEN, MICHAEL, gentleman in Cork, will, 1797. [PWI]

O'BRYON, GERTRUDE, widow in Cork, will, 1769. [PWI]

O'CONNELL, DANIEL, gentleman in Cork, will, 1722. [PWI]

O'DONOGHUE, JEFFREY, in Cork, will, 1790. [PWI]

O'DONOGHUE, ROBERT, in Cork, will, 1808. [PWI]

O'DOUGHERTY, MICHAEL, in Cork, will, 1806. [PWI]

O'LEARY, JOHN, born in Cork 1779, a merchant who was naturalised in South Carolina in 1804. [NARA.M1183]

O'MULLANE, ANDREW, gentleman in Cork, will, 1759. [PWI]

O'MULLANE, JOHN, gentleman in Cork, will, 1766. [PWI]

O'MULLANE, JOHN, gentleman in Cork, will, 1806. [PWI]

OAKMAN, ROBERT, linen-draper in Cork, will, 1768. [PWI]

OLIVER, CHRISTOPHER, alderman of Cork, will, 1690. [PWI]

OLIVER, ROBERT, and the widow Kelly, were married in Cork during October 1770. [FLJ.86]

OLIVER, THOMAS, in Cork, will, 1799. [PWI]

OSBORNE, EDWARD, of Glannekittane, gentleman in Cork city, deposition, 1641. [TCD.823.27]

OSBORNE, HENRY, MD in Cork, will, 1811. [PWI]

OSBURNE, QUENTIN, a chemist in Cork, a bond, 1704. [NRS.GD109.2390]; surgeon in Cork, will, 1750. [PWI]

OWGAN, THOMAS, Mayor of Cork in 1777. [CBC]

OWGAN, WILLIAM, Mayor of Cork in 1742. [CBC]

PARKER, HARDING, Mayor of Cork in 1740. [CBC]

PARKER, MARGARET, widow in Cork, will, 1802. [PWI]

PARME, WILLIAM, a baker in Cork, will, 1737. [PWI]

PATERSON, NICHOLAS, a shipmaster of Cork, died 1795. [Cork Courier, Vol.1, 1 April 1795]

PATTEN, LASSAIGNE, merchant in Cork, will, 1762. [PWI]

PEARSE, DANIEL, Alderman of Cork, will, 1727. [PWI]

PEDDER, BELCHER, in Cork, will, 1769. [PWI]

PEDDER, DORCAS, widow in Cork, will, 1793. [PWI]

PEDDER, JOHN, in Cork, will, 1805. [PWI]

PEEKE, Mrs, wife of Reverend Peeke minister of the French Church in Cork, died in Mallow in August 1765. [FDJ.3993]

PEIRARA, ..., in Cork, a petition, 1693. [AC]

PEIRSIE, JAMES, Customs Controller of Cork in 1626. [CPRIre]

PEISLY, ELIZABETH, widow in Cork, will, 1662. [PWI]

PEIRSY, JAMES, a merchant, died near Cork in March 1764. [FDJ.3850]

PEMBROKE, THOMAS, Mayor of Cork in 1733. [CBC]

PEMBROKE, THOMAS, in Cork, will, 1755. [PWI]

PEMBROKE, WILLIAM, gentleman in Cork, will, 1799. [PWI]

PENINGTON, MARY, widow in Cork, will, 1730. [PWI]

PENNEFATHER, MARY, widow in Cork, will, 1788. [PWI]

PERCY, JONATHAN, in Christchurch parish, Cork, in 1659. [C]

PERDRIAN, DANIEL, merchant in Cork, will, 1783. [PWI]

PERRIE, JOSEPH, a constable of the Staple of Cork in 1699. [AC]

THE PEOPLE OF CORK, 1600-1799

PERRY, RICHARD, in Cork, will, 1799. [PWI]

PHILIPS, NOBLET, Mayor of Cork in 1768. [CBC]

PHILIPS, WILLIAM, born 1694, from Liverpool to America in 1702. [LRO]

PHILPOT, USHER, Mayor of Cork in 1757. [CBC]

PHIPPS, GEORGE, in Cork, will, 1790. [PWI]

PICK, ELLINOR, widow in Cork, will, 1768. [PWI]

PICK, JOHN, born 1707, from Geneva, Switzerland, minister of the French Church in Cork in 1732. [AC]

PICK, JOHN, merchant in Cork, will, 1740. [PWI]

PICK, VESIAN, Mayor of Cork in 1796. [CBC]

PICKETT, MICHAEL, born 1768 in Cork, a seaman aboard HMS Venable, flagship of Admiral Adam Duncan, at the Battle of Camperdown on 11 October 1797. [TNA.Adm]

PIERCE, DANIEL, Mayor of Cork in 1722. [CBC]

PIERCY, GEORGE, in Cork, will, 1784. [PWI]

PIERCY, JAMES, a gentleman in Cork city, Controller of the Port of Cork, deposition, 1641. [TCD.823.108]

PIERCY, JAMES, merchant in Cork, will, 1764. [PWI]

PIERCY, JEFFREY, merchant in Cork, will, 1796. [PWI]

PIERCY, PAUL, in Cork, will, 1790. [PWI]

PIERSY, ROBERT, searcher of the port, in parish of Rathcooney, barony of Cork, deposition, 1641. [TCD.822.104]

PIERS, EDWARD, merchant in Cork, will, 1742. [PWI]

PIGOTT, GEORGE, in Cork, will, 1773. [PWI]

PIKE, ANNE, widow of Ebenezer Pike in Cork, will, 1808. [PWI]

PIKE, DEBORAH, widow in Cork, will, 1760. [PWI]

PIKE, EBENEZER, banker in Cork, will, 1785. [PWI]

PIKE, JOSEPH, merchant in Cork, will, 1729. [PWI]

PIKE, RICHARD, a Quaker, died in Cork in 1764. [FDJ.3813]; merchant in Cork, will, 1768. [PWI]

PIKE, RICHARD, banker in Cork, will, 1811. [PWI]

PIKE, SAMUEL, in Cork, will, 1797. [PWI]

PIM, SAMUEL, clothier in Cork, will, 164. [PWI]

PINCHON, THOMAS, of Ballinspeckbey, in the parish of St Finbarr's, barony of Cork, deposition, 1641. [TCD.824.34]

PLAINCE, STEPHEN, died on Coal Quay, Cork, in 1764. [FDJ.3813]

PLUNCKETT, ROBERT, born 1623 in Cork, a mariner aboard the Sampson a witness before the High Court of the Admiralty of England in 1647. [TNA.HCA.62.2]

POLDEN, HUGH, merchant in Cork, will, 1702. [PWI]

POMEROY, JOHN, Archdeacon of Cork, will, 1724. [PWI]

POOLE, FRANCIS, a clothier, died in Watergate Lane, Cork, in March 1764. [FDJ.3846]

POPE, WILLIAM, brewer in Cork, will, 1718. [PWI]

POPE, WILLIAM, merchant in Cork, will, 1738. [PWI]

POPE, WILLIAM, merchant in Cork, will, 1741. [PWI]

POWELL, GILES, gentleman in Cork, will, 1804. [PWI]

POWER, JAMES, a pilot in Cork in 1609. [AC]

POWER, RICHARD, MD, died in Castle Street, Cork, in 1764. [FDJ.3787]

POWER, WILLIAM, an apothecary, and Miss Callanan, were married in Cork during March 1764. [FDJ.3847]

PRICE, FRANCIS, merchant in Cork, will, 1765. [PWI]

PRICE, THOMAS, in Christchurch parish, Cork, in 1659. [C]

PRIDDEN, RICHARD, in Christchurch parish, Cork, in 1659. [C]

PROCTOR, JOSEPH, in Cork, a letter, 1770. [PRONI.D1044.267]

PUMPHREY, JOHN, woollen draper in Cork, will, 1766. [PWI]

PURCELL, AMY, in Cork, will, 1758. [PWI]

PURCELL, MARY, spinster in Cork, will, 1742. [PWI]

THE PEOPLE OF CORK, 1600-1799

PURCELL, RICHARD, Mayor of Cork in 1788. [CBC]

PURCELL, THOMAS, clothier in Cork, will, 1802. [PWI]

PUREFOY, WILLIAM, in Cork, will, 1797. [PWI]

PUXLEY, HENRY, Mayor of Cork in 1791. [CBC]

PYNE, JOHN, born in Cork in 1767, a planter who was naturalised in South Carolina in 1813. [NARA.M1183]

QUIN, EDWARD, in Cork, a letter, 1725. [PRONI.D2707.A1.1.7E]

RAHILL, DANIEL, born in Cork, a seaman aboard HMS Venable, flagship of Admiral Adam Duncan, at the Battle of Camperdown on 11 October 1797. [TNA.Adm]

RAWLINS, FRANCIS, jr., and Miss Minton of Cork, were married in Cork in January 1764. [FDJ.3836]

RAWLINSON, WILLIAM, died in Cork during October 1770. [FLJ.86]

RAYMOND, PHILIP, merchant in Cork, will, 1697. [PWI]

REARDEN, DENNIS, from Cork, was naturalised in South Carolina in 1798. [NARA.M1183]

REEVES, EDWARD, in Cork, will, 1811. [PWI]

REEVES, ROBERT, in Cork, will, 1806. [PWI]

REILY, JOHN, Mayor of Cork in 1755. [CBC]

RICE, MARY, widow in Cork, will, 1737. [PWI]

THE PEOPLE OF CORK, 1600-1799

RICE, THOMAS FITZMARCUS, a merchant in Cork, will, 1733. [PWI]

RICH, RICHARD, in Christchurch parish, Cork, in 1659. [C]

RICHMOND, THOMAS, a gentleman in Cork, will, 1807. [PWI]

RING, WILIAM, born 1767 in Cork, a seaman aboard HMS Venable, flagship of Admiral Adam Duncan, at the Battle of Camperdown on 11 October 1797. [TNA.Adm]

ROBBERTS, HODDER, a gentleman in Cork, will, 1719. [PWI]

ROBERTS, CATHERINE, a widow in Cork, will, 1770. [PWI]

ROBERTS, THOMAS, a clerk, in the parish of St Finbarr's, barony of Cork, deposition, 1641. [TCD.824.249]

ROBERTS, THOMAS, a banker in Cork, will, 1801. [PWI]

ROBERTS, Mrs, wife of Captain Nicholas Roberts, in the West India trade, died on the Mall, Cork, in Sept. 1765. [FDJ.4010]

ROBINETT, WILLIAM, a merchant in Cork, will, 1807. [PWI]

ROCH, CHRISTIAN, a widow, 'an ancient native and inhabitant of Cork' petitioned King Charles II in 1670. [CSP.Dom.Signet Office VII, 382[]

ROCHE, EDMOND, in Cork, will, 1750. [DRD]

ROCHE, FRANCIS, 'an ancient native and inhabitant of Cork' petitioned King Charles II in 1670. [CSP.Dom.Signet Office VII, 382]

THE PEOPLE OF CORK, 1600-1799

ROCHE, FRANCIS, a coach-maker in Cork, will, 1754. [PWI]

ROCHE, JANET, a widow in Cork, 1609. [CBC]

ROCHE, JOHN, born 1602 in Cork, a merchant, a witness before the High Court of the Admiralty of England in 1627. [TNA.HCA.46.386]

ROCHE, MORRISH FITZGERALD, a merchant in Cork, will, 1655. [PWI]

ROCHE, MORRIS, in Cork, a Roman Catholic, licensed to bear arms in 1705. [HMS.Ormonds.11.476]

ROCH, PATRICK, was appointed Sergeant of Cork in 1609. [AC]

ROCH, PATRICK, 'an ancient native and inhabitant of Cork' petitioned King Charles II in 1670. [CSP.Dom.Signet Office VII, 382]

ROCHFORT, DAVID, a merchant in Cork, will, 1733. [PWI]

ROCHFORT, DAVID, in Cork, will, 1811. [PWI]

ROE, Captain JOHN, died in his house in George's Street, Cork, in September 1765. [FDJ.4003]

ROE, JOHN, Mayor of Cork in 1772. [CBC]; will, 1780. [PWI]

ROGERS, BAYLEY, in Cork, will, 1786. [PWI]

ROGERS, HANNAH, in Cork, will, 1728. [PWI]

ROGERS, HENRY, in Cork, will, 1774. [PWI]

ROGERS, JOANNA, a widow in Cork, will, 1807. [PWI]

ROGERS, JOSEPH, in Cork, will, 1757. [PWI]

ROGERS, JOSEPH, in Cork, a mortgage, 1792. [PRONI.D2464.4.2]; will, 1801. [PWI]

ROGERS, NOBLETT, in Cork, will, 1780. [PWI]

ROGERS, ROBERT, in Cork, his will refers to his sons George and Christopher, cousin Robert Rogers, grandsons Noblet Rogers jr. and George Rogers jr sons of alderman Noblet Rogers, Robert Rogers, Corsely Rogers. Francis Roger, Richard Rogers sons of the late Francis Rogers, nephews Robert and William Rogers both gentlemen in Ashgrove, County Cork, Richard Nason a tenant, Herbert Love a lessee, Peter Sargent, John Pomphrey, alderman Edward Browne, alderman Edward Hoare, Mary Maliburne alias Lamley, Denis Fling, Thomas Baker, Patrick Magh, Denis Morphey a boatman, John Ralph and Thomas Mitchell; witnesses Reverend Cornelius Hignet. Edmond and Thomas Barry both scriveners in Cork, and William Masters, probate 6 November 1718. [DRD]

ROGERS, ROBERT, in Cork, will, 1800. [PWI]

ROGERS, WILLIAM, in Cork, will, 1800. [PWI]

RONEUEN, JAMES, in Cork, a petition, 1693. [AC]

RONANE, EDMUND, 'an ancient native and inhabitant of Cork' petitioned King Charles II in 1670. [CSP.Dom.Signet VII, 382]

RONAN, JAMES, in Cork, pardoned in 1628. [CPRIre]

RONAN, JAMES, 'an ancient native and inhabitant of Cork' petitioned King Charles II in 1670. [CSP.Dom.Signet VII, 382]

RONAN, MORRIS, in Cork, pardoned in 1628. [CPRIre]

RONAN, THOMAS, in Cork, pardoned in 1628. [CPRIre]

RONEUEN, JAMES, in Cork, a petition, 1693. [AC]

ROSE, THOMAS, a gentleman in Cork, will, 1629. [PWI]

ROSS, HONORA, a widow in Cork, will, 1781. [PWI]

ROSS, ROBERT, a vintner in Cork, will, 1773. [PWI]

ROWLAND, EDWARD, Major of the Cork city's Royal Regiment of Militia, will, 1803. [PWI]

ROULAND, FRANCIS, Mayor of Cork in 1773. [CBC]

ROWLAND, SAMUEL, Mayor of Cork in 1786. [CBC]

ROYNANE, Mrs MARY, died in Cork in June 1765. [FDJ.3983]

RUDDOCK, JOSEPH, master of the Hannah of Cork from Jamaica to Bristol in 1705. [TNA.SP63.365.267]

RUSSELL, JOHN, a merchant in Cork, will, 1800. [PWI]

RUSSELL, THOMAS, Archdeacon of Cork, will, 1745. [PWI]

RYAN, JOHN, a merchant in Cork, will, 1800. [PWI]

RYAN, WILLIAM, a merchant, died in Cork in 1766. [FDJ.4085]

RYE, JOHN, eldest son of George Rye, was admitted as a Freeman of Cork in 1741. [CBC]

SADLEIR, CLEMENT, a master cooper in Cork, will, 1803. [PWI]

SAINT LAWRENCE, THOMAS, Bishop of Cork, will, 1805. [PWI]

SAINT LEGER, HAYWARD, in Cork, will, 1688. [PWI]

SAINT LEGER, HAYWARD, in Cork, will, 1799. [PWI]

SAINT LEGER, JOHN, in Cork, will, 1730. [PWI]

SAINT LEGER, WARHAM, in Cork, will, 1784. [PWI]

SAINT LEGER, WILLIAM, a merchant in Cork, will, 1741. [PWI]

SANDIFORD, JAMES, in Cork, will, 1804. [PWI]

SARLSFIELD, Reverend, born 1660, died in Cork in 1766. [SM.28.615][FDJ.4126]

SARSFIELD, CATHERINE, relict of Dominick Sarsfield, died in Cork in 1766. [FDJ.4118]

SARSFIELD, DOMINICK, 'an ancient native and inhabitant of Cork' petitioned Charles II in 1670. [CSP.Dom.Signet VII, 382]

SARSFIELD, DOMINICK, in Cork, will, 1764. [PWI]

SARSFIELD, IGNATIUS, MD, from Cork, was admitted as a citizen of Rotterdam, Zealand, on 11 December 1792; he married Agatha Gezant from Hertenbosch, North Brabant, in Rotterdam on 12 September 1785. [GAR]

SARSFIELD, MARY, a widow in Cork, will, 1802. [PWI]

SARSFIELD, PATRICK, 'an ancient native and inhabitant of Cork' petitioned King Charles II in 1670. [CSP.Dom.Signet Office VII, 382]

SARSFIELD, THOMAS, in Cork, will, 1751. [PWI]

SARSFIELD, WILLIAM, in Cork in 1609. [AC]

SAVAGE, RICHARD, in Christchurch, Cork, in 1659. [C]

SAUNDERS, REBECCA, a widow in Cork, will, 1791. [PWI]

SAUNDERS, Mrs, a widow, died in Cork in August 1770. [FLJ.63]

SCOTT, EDWARD, of Mallow Lane, Cork, a clothier, married Harriot Williamson, daughter of Captain Williamson deceased, in December 1766. [FDJ.4137]

SCOTT, RICHARD, a gentleman in Cork, will, 1801. [PWI]

SCUDDAMORE, RICHARD, Customs officer in Cork, 1666. CSPIre.1666]

SCULLAY, JEREMIAH, born 1770 in Cork, a seaman aboard HMS Venable, flagship of Admiral Adam Duncan, at the Battle of Camperdown on 11 October 1797. [TNA.Adm]

SCULLY, JOHN SULLIVAN, born 1768, a merchant in Cork, with his wife Mary Scully, born 1775, emigrated from Cork on 1 September 1803 aboard the Fortitude of New York, master Hezekia Pinkham, bound for New York. [BM]

SEAGRAVE, Mr, a teacher of the French language, died near South Gate, Cork, in May 1765. [FDJ.3969]

SEALY, JOHN, in Cork, will, 1720. [PWI]

SHARPE, JOHN, in Christchurch parish, Cork, in 1659. [C]

SHAWE, BERNARD, Collector of the Port of Cork, will, 1808. [PWI]

SHAW, JOHN, Mayor of Cork in 1792. [CBC]; will, 1807. [PWI]

SHEA, ANDREW, from Cork, was admitted as a citizen of Rotterdam, Zealand, on 15 April 1779. [GAR]

SHEA, GEORGE, a merchant in Cork, will, 1811. [PWI]

SHEA, HENRY, from Cork, was admitted as a citizen of Rotterdam, Zealand, on 11 December 1773. [GAR]

SHEA, JOHN, a merchant in Cork, will, 1790. [PWI]

SHEA, LUKE, a cooper, and Margaret Mulcahy, were married in Cork on in June 1770. [FLJ.49]

SHEANE, THOMAS, of Knockorgen, Cork city, deposition, 1641. [TCD.825.284]

SHEARS, HENRY, in Cork, will, 1750. [PWI]

SHEARES, THOMAS, a gentleman in Cork, will refers to his kinsman Henry Sheares, his father Humphrey Sheares, aunt Jane, aunt Mary Lye, cousins Charles Newman and Mary Wright, kinsman Sheares Olliffe, Charles Newman a gentleman in Cork, Thomas Browne an apothecary in Cork, godson

Richard Browne, god-daughter Sheares Browne daughter of Richard Browne of Dundarricke, Elinor Sweeny, William Love, Christopher Love, Elizabeth Dickson, Mary Olliffe, Elizabeth Wade, Dorothy Skippen, Thomas Deane a servant; witnesses John and Francis Roche, James Crooke, William Chartres jr., Nathaniel Barry, Charles Callaghan, and Charles Whiting, probate 8 May 1717. [DRD]

SHEEHAN, CATHERINE, 'a poor woman who had long labored under a dropsy, for which she had been tapped 97 times since the month of June 1760', died in Cork in August 1765. [FDJ.3999]

SHEEHAN, JEREMIAH, a nurseryman in Cork, will, 1781. [PWI]

SHEEHY, BRYAN, in Cork, will, 1808. [PWI]

SHEEHY, ROGER, in Cork, will, 1797. [PWI]

SHEEHY, WILLIAM, a merchant in Cork, will, 1783. [PWI]

SHEPPARD, JOHN, in Cork, letters, 1714, 1715, 1716, 1719. [TCD.750.1558/1568/1573/1615/1755/1761/1901]

SHINNICK, Mrs MARY, born 1717, died at Clerk's Bridge in Cork in 1821. [SM.87.191]

SHORTON, JOHN, born 1782, a carpenter from Cork, was naturalised in South Carolina in 1813. [NARA.M1183]

SHOWLAND, DANIEL, from Cork, emigrated via Liverpool aboard the Ann and Sarah bound for America in 1697. [LRO]

SIMMONS, ISAAC, in Cork, will, 1792. [PWI]

SIMPSON, GEORGE, a gentleman in Cork, will, 1721. [PWI]

SINCLAIR, JAMES, in Cork Gaol, a letter, 1758. [NRS.GD136.398]

SINDERBEE, RICHARD, a merchant in Cork, will, 1771. [PWI]

SKEYS, WILLIAM, a merchant, formerly an apprentice to Benjamin Winthrop, was admitted as a Freeman of Cork in 1741. [CBC]

SKIDDY, GEORGE, 'an ancient native and inhabitant of Cork' petitioned King Charles II in 1670. [CSP.Dom.Signet Office VII, 382]

SKIDDY, THOMAS, in Cork, a bond, 1637. [PRONI.D430.142]

SLEE, JOSEPH, from Cork, was admitted as a citizen of Rotterdam, Zealand, on 17 September 1720. [GAR]

SMART, HENRY, yeoman, in the parish of St Finbarr's, barony of Cork, deposition, 1641. [TCD.824.140]

SMART, WILLIAM, of Synane, a yeoman in Cork city, deposition, 1641. [TCD.825.303]

SMART, WILLIAM, a gentleman in Cork, will, 1683. [PWI]

SMITH, BRYAN, a saddler on Hammond's Marsh, and Catherine Magrath, daughter of John Magrath a merchant tailor on Castle Street, were married in Cork in July 1770. [FLJ.55]

SMITH, FURLONG, a merchant in Cork, will, 1808. [PWI]

SMITH, HENRY, born 1765, a ships carpenter from Cork, was naturalised in South Carolina in 1807. [NARA.M1183]

SMITH, Captain JAMES, and Mary Warren, were married in Cork during July 1770. [FLJ.61]

SMITH, JOHN, Mayor of Cork in 1763. [CBC]; will, 1775. [PWI]

SMITH, JOHN, a cooper in Cork, will, 1777. [PWI]

SMITH, MARY, of Gill Abbey, in the parish of St Finbarr's, barony of Cork, deposition, 1641. [TCD.822.281]

SMITH, MATHIAS, a gentleman in Cork, will refers to the six grandchildren, the children of his deceased son Mathias Smith – Mathias Smith, John Smith, Baptist Smith, Jane Smith, Catherine Smith, and Elizabeth Smith, his three grandchildren, children of Nathaniel Harvey deceased – John Harvey, Katherine Harvey, and Mary Harvey, his daughter Anne wife of Anthony Goss, and daughter Mary Harvey, grandson Mathias son of Baptist Smith deceased, sister Elizabeth Patch, sister Susanna Mather, friend John Allin an alderman, cousin John Sullivan a gentleman in Cork, William Oliffe a shopkeeper Cork, Mrs Mary Pennington, an apprentice Stephen Trustram,his old servant John Morris; witnesses William Chartres jr., Cornelius Lyne and Thomas Barry, .probate 13 November 1719. [DRD]

SMITH, MATHIAS, Mayor of Cork in 1752. [CBC]

SMITHWICK, MICHAEL, in Cork, will, 1809. [PWI]

SOFTLAW, JOHN, a merchant in Cork, will, 1761. [PWI]

SPAIGHT, PAULMS, married Miss Lane, daughter of William Lane of Cork, there in October 1765. [FDJ.4012]

SPENSER, SAMUEL, a merchant in Cork, will, 1795. [PWI]

SPENCER, THOMAS, of Gortaglane, in the parish of St Finbarr's, barony of Cork, deposition, 1641. [TCD.822.244]

SPITAL, JOHN, Lieutenant Colonel of the 47th Regiment of Foot, commanded by Lieutenant General Peregrine Lascelles, died in Cork in March 1765. [FDJ.3952]

SPIRES, Mrs, wife of Thomas Spires, died in Cork in July 1765. [FDJ.3988]

SPREAD, MELIAN, a spinster in Cork, will, 1758. [PWI]

STACK, WILLIAM, and Jane Lindsay, were married in Cork during October 1770. [FLJ.82]

STAVELLY, ROBERT, a merchant in Cork, will, 1795. [PWI]

STERLING, LUKE, of Cork City, will dated 13 November 1766, proved 30 May 1769. Refers to his wife Elizabeth, their only son Marlborough Parsons Sterling. His brother Parsons Sterling and his son James. His sister Isabella Saint Clare and her sons Edward and William. Dated 13 November 1766, proved 30 May 1769. [DRD]

STERNE, ELIZABETH, a widow in Cork, will, 1739. [PWI]

STEWART, ANNESLEY, in Cork, a deed, 1769. [PRONI.D2358.1.8]

STEWART, JAMES, in Cork, a letter, 1798. [NRAS.2177.Bundle 5326]

STEWART, MARY, born 1748, a gentlewoman in Cork, emigrated from Cork on 1 September 1803 aboard the Fortitude of New York, master Hezekia Pinkham, bound for New York. [BM]

STIFFE, ARON, in Christchurch parish, Cork, in 1659. [C]

STOCKDALE, SUSANNA, a widow in Cork, will, 1769. [PWI]

STOKES, PATRICK, a merchant in Cork, will, 1765. [PWI]

STOKES, ROBERT, a merchant in Cork, will, 1779. [PWI]

STOTHARD, THOMAS, a peuterer in Cork, will, 1707. [PWI]

STOUGHTON, ANTHONY, in Cork, will, 1644. [PWI]

STRETTELL, AMOS, a merchant in Cork, will, 1795. [PWI]

STRITCH, GEORGE, a merchant in Cork, will, 1747. [PWI]

STRITCH, MARY, daughter of James Stritch a merchant in Cork, married Richard England a merchant, in Limerick, during February 1764. [FDJ.3842]

STUART, HENRY, was granted property in Cork in 1646 which his son and heir William Stuart claimed on 12 August 1657. [CSPI.1657.844]

SULLIVAN, JOHN, from Cork, was admitted as a citizen of Rotterdam, Zealand, on 5 September 1719. [GAR]

SULLIVAN, MICHAEL, a vintner, died in Cork during September 1770. [FLJ.73]

SULLIVAN, ..., died in Blarney Lane, Cork, in July 1770. [FLJ.61]

SWABBY, THOMAS, in Christchurch parish, Cork, in 1659. [C]

SWALLOW, THOMAS, in Christchurch parish, Cork, 1659. [C]

SWANTON, JOHN, born 1775 in Cork, naturalised in New York in 1810. [NWI.II.247]

SWAYNE, HUGH, a merchant in Cork, will, 1760. [PWI]

SWEENEY, JOHN, a cooper, was admitted as a Freeman of Cork in 1770. [CCCA]

SWEENY, BRYAN, from Cork, was naturalised in South Carolina in 1796. [NARA.M1183]

SWEET, HENRY, a gentleman, was appointed joint searcher, packer, and gauger of Cork by King James II in 168-. [AC]

SWEET, JOHN, former apprentice to Sheriff Winthrop, was a Freeman of Corn in 1741; Mayor of Cork in 1758. [CBC]

SWINNEY, EDWARD, a cooper, was admitted as a Freeman of Cork in 1780. [CCCA]

SWINEY, EUGENE, a printer and book-seller, and Miss Callanan, were married in Cork in 1766. [FDJ.4069]

SWINEY, JAMES, a printer, died in Cork in 1763. [FDJ.3815]

SWINEY, JOHN, born 1776 in Cork, naturalised in New York in 1805. [NWI.II.245]

SYMPSON, JOHN, a gentleman, was admitted as a Freeman of Cork in 1762. [CCCA]

SYNGE, EDWARD, Bishop of Cork, will, 1678. [PWI]

SYNGE, BARBARA, widow of the Bishop of Cork, will, 1712. [PWI]

TANNER, ELIZABETH, born in America, in Cork, will, 1805. [PWI]

TARRANT, PHILIP, a cooper, was admitted as a Freeman of Cork in 1783. [CCCA]

TAYLOR, ANNE, a widow in Cork, will, 1770. [PWI]

TAYLOR, BERKLEY, a merchant in Cork, son of William Taylor a merchant of Burton, County Cork, and Sarah Hoare, daughter of Edward Hoare in Hatherley, Somerset, England, a marriage settlement, 1698. [PRONI.D778.21]

TAYLOR, ELIZABETH, a widow in Cork, will, 1826. [PWI; Hawkins]

TAYLOR, FRANCIS, a silversmith, was admitted as a Freeman of Cork in 1761. [CCCA]

TAYLOR, ISRAEL, a clerk, in the parish of St Finbarr's, barony of Cork, deposition, 1641. [TCD.825.294]

TAYLOR, JOHN, a clothier, was admitted as a Freeman of Cork in 1761. [CCCA]

TAYLOR, THOMAS, a merchant, was admitted as a Freeman of Cork in 1740. [CCCA]

TAYLOR, WILLIAM, Mayor of Cork in 1746. [CBC]

TAYLOR, WILLIAM, in Cork, will, 1761. [PWI]

TAYLOR, WILLIAM, a tallow chandler, was admitted as a Freeman of Cork in 1764. [CCCA]

TERRY, CARDEN, a silversmith, was admitted as a Freeman of Cork in 1785. [CCCA]

TERRY, JAMES, of Castle Terry, died in Cork during June 1770. [FLJ.51]

TERRY. JOHN, in Christchurch parish, Cork, in 1659. [C]

TERRY, RICHARD, in Christchurch parish, Cork, in 1659. [C]

TERRY, WILLIAM, in Cork, was granted Derryallen in County Cork in 1627. [CPRIre]

TENT, Lieutenant JOHN, in Cork, will, 1663. [PWI]

TEULON, JOHN, a merchant, was admitted as a Freeman of Cork in 1775. [CCCA]

THIRRY, DAVID, 'an ancient native and inhabitant of Cork' petitioned King Charles II in 1670. [CSP.Dom.Signet Office VII, 382]

THE PEOPLE OF CORK, 1600-1799

THOMAS, DANIEL, born 1679, a laborer, died in Glanmire, Cork, in 1787. [SM.49.518]

THOMAS, JAMES, a cooper, was admitted as a Freeman of Cork in 1792. [CCCA]

THOMAS, JOHN, and Miss Lynch, were married in Cork during October 1770. [FLJ.83]

THOMAS, THOMAS, a cooper, was admitted as a Freeman of Cork in 1782. [CCCA]

THOMAS, WILLIAM, a gentleman in Cork, will, 1783. [PWI]

THOMPSON, ARCHIBALD DOUGLAS, a sail-cloth weaver in Cork, will, 1787. [PWI]

THOMPSON, JOHN, a merchant, was admitted as a Freeman of Cork in 1763. [CCCA]

THOMPSON, JOHN, Mayor of Cork in 1794. [CBC]

THOMPSON, PARR, a gentleman, was admitted as a Freeman of Cork in 1763. [CCCA]

THRESHER, MARY, widow of Daniel Thresher a merchant in Cork, will, 1744. [PWI]

THYNNE, Captain EDWARD, Governor and Constable of Cork Castle in 1623. [CPRIre]

TIRRY, EDMUND, a burgess of Cork in 1613. [SPIre]

TISDAL, Reverend GEORGE, DD, was admitted as a Freeman of Cork in 1752. [CCCA]

TISDAL, PETER, a merchant, was admitted as a Freeman of Cork in 1751. [CCCA]

TOBIN, RICHARD, born 1770 in Cork, a seaman aboard HMS Venable, flagship of Admiral Adam Duncan, at the Battle of Camperdown on 11 October 1797. [TNA.Adm]

TORRY, SARAH, a widow in Cork, will, 1767. [PWI]

TOTTENHAM, CLIFFE, in Cork, will, 1773. [PWI]

TOUCHSTONE, HENRY, a merchant, was admitted as a Freeman of Cork in 1773. [CCCA]

TOWGOOD, GEORGE, in Cork, will, 1720. [PWI]

TOWGOOD, SAMPSON, in Cork, will, 1760. [PWI]

TOWNSHEND, HORATIO, a Justice of the Peace, died in Cork in February 1764. [FDJ.3844]

TOWNSEND, Reverend HORACE, in Cork, a letter, 1786. [PRONI.D2707.A.2.2.86]

TOWNSHEND, Mrs, wife of Richard Townshend a knight of the shire of Cork, died in Cork in December 1765. [FDJ.4029]

TOWNSEND, RICHARD, Member of Parliament for Cork, was admitted as a Freeman of Cork in 1765. [CCCA]

TOWNSEND, RICHARD, MD, was admitted as a Freeman of Cork in 1784. [CCCA]

TRACY, MCGEORGE, and Betty Williams, were married in Cork during October 1770. [FLJ.83]

TRANT, DOMINICK, was admitted as a Freeman of Cork in 1780. [CCCA]

TRANT, WILLIAM, a merchant in Cork, will, 1725. [PWI]

TRANTER, JAMES, Apparitor General of the Diocese of Waterford and Lismore, died in Cork during June 1770. [FLJ.52]

TRAVERS, BOYLE, a merchant, was admitted as a Freeman of Cork in 1743. [CCCA]

TRAVERS, BOYLE, Mayor of Cork in 1764. [CBC]; died at New Bank, Cork, in 1766. [FDJ.4090]

TRAVERS, FRANCIS, a gentleman, was admitted as a Freeman of Cork in 1770. [CCCA]

TRAVERS, JANE, of Bandon, married Major Campbell, in Cork in November 1783. [WHM.616]

TRAVERS, JOHN, a merchant, was admitted as a Freeman of Cork in 1747. [CCCA]

TRAVERS, JOHN, Mayor of Cork in 1774. [CBC]

TRAVERS, JONAS, a gentleman, was admitted as a Freeman of Cork in 1759. [CCCA]

TRAVERS, JONAS, a gentleman, was admitted as a Freeman of Cork in 1790. [CCCA]

TRAVERS, ROBERT, an attorney, was admitted as a Freeman of Cork in 1786. [CCCA]

THE PEOPLE OF CORK, 1600-1799

TRAVERS, ROBERT, a gentleman in Abbey Street, was admitted as a Freeman of Cork in 1788. [CCCA]

TRAVERS, WALTER, was admitted as a Freeman of Cork in 1758. [CCCA]; Mayor of Cork in 1781. [CBC]

TRAVERS, WILLIAM, eldest son of Edward Travers, was admitted as a Freeman of Cork in 1741. [CBC]

TRAVERS, WILLIAM, a mariner, was admitted as a Freeman of Cork in 1776. [CCCA]

TRAVERS, Mrs, relict of Edward Travers, died in William Street, Cork, in February 1864. [FDJ.3837]

TRAYOR, ABBOT, a gentleman, was admitted as a Freeman of Cork in 1788. [CCCA]

TRENCH, ROBERT, a judge, was admitted as a Freeman of Cork in 1747. [CCCA]

TRESHER, DANIEL, a merchant in Cork, will, 1738. [PWI]

TRINDALL, JAMES, died in Cork during November 1770. [FLJ.90]

TRINDER, WILLIAM, a clothier, was admitted as a Freeman of Cork in 1775. [CCCA]

TUCKEY, ANNE, a spinster in Cork, will, 1776. [PWI]

TUCKER, DAVYS, in Cork, a deed, 1769. [PRONI.D2358.1.8]

TUCKEY, DAVIS, a gentleman, was admitted as a Freeman of Cork in 1798. [CCCA]

TUCKEY, FRANCIS, a gentleman in Cork, will, 1745. [PWI]

TUCKEY, JANE, a spinster in Cork, will, 1767. [PWI]

TUCKEY, JOHN, a surgeon in Cork, will, 1762. [PWI]

TUCKEY, TIMOTHY, an MD in Cork, will, 1767. [PWI]

TUCKEY, STEARNE, a gentleman, was admitted as a Freeman of Cork in 1734. [CCCA]; will, 1785. [PWI]

TUCKEY, THOMAS, a merchant in Cork, will, 1737. [PWI]

TUCKEY, THOMAS, of Cork, and .... Kingston, daughter of Reverend Kingston of Kilpadder, were married in August 1770. [FLJ.70]

TUCKEY, THOMAS, a gentleman, was admitted as a Freeman of Cork in 1782. [CCCA]

TUCKEY, TIMOTHY, in Christchurch parish, Cork, in 1659. [C]

TUCKEY, TIMOTHY, jr., in Christchurch parish, Cork, 1659. [C]

TUCKEY, TIMOTHY, the Mayor of Cork and later an Alderman, 1686. [AC]

TURGES, JOSEPH, eldest son of Andrew Turges, was admitted as a Freeman of Cork in 1716. [CCCA]

TURNER, JOHN, a glazier, was admitted as a Freeman of Cork in 1775. [CCCA]

TURVIN, JAMES, was admitted as a Freeman of Cork in 1735. [CCCA]

TURVIN, WILLIAM, a gentleman, was admitted as a Freeman of Cork in 1776. [CCCA]

TWOGOOD, GEORGE, a tinplate worker in Cork, will, 1800. [PWI]

TYDD, FRANCIS, a gentleman, was admitted as a Freeman of Cork in 1766. [CCCA]; will, 1796. [PWI]

TYDD, FRANCIS, a gentleman, was admitted as a Freeman of Cork in 1777. [CCCA]

TYDD, JOHN, a gentleman, was admitted as a Freeman of Cork in 1775 [CCCA]

TYDD, ROBERT, a gentleman, was admitted as a Freeman of Cork in 1758. [CCCA]

TYRRY, DOMINIC, the Sheriff of Cork, a petition in 1611. [SPIre]

TYRRIE, DOMINICK FITZJAMES, a merchant in Cork, will, 1631. [PWI]

TYRRY, Captain DOMINICK, in Cork, will, 1690. [PWI]

TYRRYE, JOHN FITZFRANCIS, a merchant in Cork, will, 1629. [PWI]

UNIAKE, WILLIAM, a merchant, was admitted as a Freeman of Cork in 1751. [CCCA]

UNMUSSIG, JOHN, born in Nassau Dillonburg, Germany, an MD in Cork, will, 1676. [PWI]

UNTHANK, JOHN, a merchant, was admitted as a Freeman of Cork in 1794. [CCCA]

UPPINGTON, HENRY, a merchant, was admitted as a Freeman of Cork in 1792 [CCCA]

UPPINGTON, ZEBULON, a merchant, was admitted as a Freeman of Cork in 1773. [CCCA]

UPTON, ANNE, a spinster in Cork, will, 1792. [PWI]

UPTON, GILES, a cooper, was admitted as a Freeman of Cork in 1752. [CCCA]

UPTON, RUBY, a merchant, was admitted as a Freeman of Cork in 1763. [CCCA]

UPTON, SAMUEL, a gentleman, was admitted as a Freeman of Cork in 1771 [CCCA]

UVEDALE, HUGH, a clothier, was admitted as a Freeman of Cork in 1774. [CCCA]

UVEDALE, JOHN, a gentleman, was admitted as a citizen of Cork in 1773 [CCCA]; will, 1790. [PWI]

UVEDALE, RALPH, a gentleman, was admitted as a Freeman of Cork in 1752. [CCCA]

VAN DE LEUR, MARY, a widow in Cork, will, 1787. [PWI]

VEALE, JOHN, was admitted as a Freeman of Cork in 1731. [CCCA]

VERBURG, JEREMIAS, from Cork, and Pieternelletje Franse from Delftshaven, Rotterdam, were married in the Reformed

Church in Rotterdam, Zealand, on 30 October 1714. [GAR]

VERDILLE, JAMES, was admitted as a Freeman of Cork in 1723. [CCCA]

VERDON, NICHOLAS, Petty Porter at the South Gate of Cork in 1609. [AC]

VEREKER, HENRY, a gentleman in Cork, will, 1692. [PWI]

VERLING, WILLIAM, a gentleman, son of Councillor Verling, and Elizabeth Gray, daughter of Joseph Gray, were married in Cork during October 1770. [FLJ.88]

VERNALL, JOHN, a mariner in Cork, will, 1720. [PWI]

VERNON, HENRY, a gentleman, a juryman of Cork in 1609. [AC]

VOSTER, ANNE, a widow in Cork, will, 1766. [PWI]

VOSTER, DANIEL, in Cork, will, 1761. [PWI]

WADE, LUCRETIA, a spinster in Cork, will, 1807. [PWI]

WADE, THOMAS, a merchant in Cork, will, 1746. [PWI]

WAGGET, CHRISTOPHER, in Cork, will, 1796. [PWI]

WALDRON, LYDIA, a widow in Cork, will, 1795. [PWI]

WALKER, ANNE, a spinster in Cork, will, 1789. [PWI]

WALKER, FRANCIS, in Cork, will, 1797. [PWI]

WALKER, JOSIAS, in Christchurch parish, Cork, in 1659. [C]

WALL, CATHERINE, a widow in Cork, will, 1786. [PWI]

WALLER, ROBERT, MP for Dundalk and Surveyor General of Connaught, married Catherine, second daughter of the late Rev. Mr Moore of Innishannon, in Cork, 1766. [FDJ.4064]

WALLIS, BARAKY, married Miss Pigott, daughter of the late Emanuel Pigott, at St Finbarry's, Cork, in 1763. [FDJ.3822]

WALLIS, JAMES, in Cork, will, 1800. [PWI]

WALLIS, JOHN, born 1783, from Cork, a grocer in Charleston, naturalised in South Carolina in 1826. [NARA.M1183]

WALLIS, THOMAS, a gentleman in Cork, will, 1741. [PWI]

WALSH, EDMOND, mason in Cork, will, 1771. [PWI]

WALSH, EDWARD, in Cork, will, 1793. [PWI]

WALSH, Dr RICHARD, titular Bishop of Cork, died there on 6 January 1763. [SM.25.59]

WALTER, ADRIEN, a gentleman and a juryman in 1609. [AC]

WARE, HENRY, in the parish of Rathcooney, barony of Cork, deposition, 1641. [TCD.823.92]

WARNER, ANNE, a spinster in Cork, will, 1743. [PWI]

WARREN, JAMES, born 1786 in Cork, a rigger in Charleston, naturalised in South Carolina in 1827. [NARA.M1183]

WARREN, JOHN, in Cork, will, 1800. [PWI]

WARREN, Sir R., born 1724, a baronet, died in Cork in 1811. [SM.73.960]

WARREN, ..., son of John Warren jr, died in Cork during June 1770. [FLJ.53]

WATERS, DOMINICK, a merchant in Cork, will, 1792. [PWI]

WATERS, ELLINOR, a widow in Cork, will, 1812. [PWI]

WATERS, JANE, a spinster in Cork, will, 1811. [PWI]

WATKINS, ABRAHAM, in Cork, will refers to his wife Mary, daughters Mary, Ann, Sarah, and Amy, sons Richard and Abraham; witnesses Daniel Gibbs a gentleman, John Allin an alderman, William Alwin a gentleman, all of Cork, Thomas Barry, probate 4 May 1719, [DRD]

WATTS, ANTHONY, in the parish of St Finbarr's, barony of Cork, deposition, 1641. [TCD.823.105]

WEBB, JOHN, Mayor of Cork in 1771. [CBC]

WEBBER, EDWARD, in Christchurch parish, Cork, in 1659. [C]

WEBBER, EDWARD, in Cork, will, 1730. [PWI]

WEBBER, ELIZABETH, a spinster in Cork, will, 1780. [PWI]

WEBBER, GEORGE, in Christchurch parish, Cork, in 1659. [C]; in Cork in July 1670. [CSPI.328.42]; a merchant in Cork, will, 1674. [PWI]

WEBBER, GEORGE, in Cork, will, 1772. [PWI]

WEBBER, MICHAEL, a gentleman in Cork, will, 1749. [PWI]

WEEKES, ANN, a widow in Cork, will, 1783. [PWI]

WEEKES, Reverend JAMES, married Miss Hughes, daughter of John Hughes, at St Paul's church in Cork in September 1765. [FDJ.4008]

WEEKES, MARY, a widow in Cork, will, 1772. [PWI]

WEEKES, NICHOLAS, a counsellor at law in Cork, will, 1762. [PWI]

WELSH, JOHN, in Cork City, deposition, 1641. [TCD.824.228]

WELSTEAD, CHRISTIAN, a widow in Cork, will, 1771. [PWI]

WEST, GEORGE, an upholsterer, and Sarah Good, were married in Cork in August 1770. [FLJ.66]

WESTROP, PALMS, Mayor of Cork in 1778. [CBC]

WESTROP, RALPH, MD, in Cork, will, 1772. [PWI]

WESTROP, RANDAL, Mayor of Cork in 1743. [CBC]

WETENHALL, EDWARD, in Cork, will, 1732. [PWI]

WETHERALL, BENJAMIN, a clothier in Cork, will, 1742. [PWI]

WETHERALL, JOSEPH, alderman of Cork, will, 1788. [PWI]

WHEDDON, HANNAH, a widow in Cork, will, 1774. [PWI]

WHEELER, ROBERT, master of an English vessel, died in Cork in June 1770. [FLJ.50]

WHEELER, SARAH, a widow in Cork, will, 1766. [PWI]

WHEELER, WILLIAM, in the parish of St Finbarr's, barony of Cork, deposition, 1641. [TCD.825.276]

WHEELER, WILLIAM, a merchant in Cork, will, 1752. [PWI]

WHEELER, Mrs, died in Cork in March 1765, 'supposed to be occasioned by being in liquor'. [FDJ.3952]

WHELAN, JOHN, died in Cork during October 1770. [FLJ.83]

WHETCROFT, HENRY, a yeoman, in the parish of St Finbarr's, barony of Cork, deposition, 1641. [TCD.823.181]

WHITBY, Captain MARCUS, in Fermoy, Cork, probate 1660 PCC. [TNA]

WHITE, EPHRAIM, a gentleman in Cork, will, 1805. [PWI]

WHITE, JAMES, born 1782, from Cork, was naturalised in South Carolina in 1814. [NARA.M1183]

WHITE, JOSHUA, in Cork, will, 1800. [PWI]

WHITE, Miss MARY, died on the Mall, Cork, in 1763. [FDJ.3819]

WHITE, STEPHEN, a merchant in Cork, will, 1793. [PWI]

WHITE, THOMAS, a clerk in Cork, will, 1778. [PWI]

WHITE, THOMAS, a stationer in Cork, will, 1803. [PWI]

WHITE, WILLIAM, died in Cork, 1766. [FDJ.4043]

WHYTE, Mr, married Miss Foley, in Cork in February 1765. [FDJ.3944]

WHITING, JOHN, master of the Joseph of Cork in 1691. [ActsPCCol.1691.364/55]

WHITNEY, RICHARD, a gunsmith, died in Cork in 1766. [FDJ.4101]

WIGHT, JOHN, a merchant in Cork, will, 1759. [PWI]

WILLCOCKS, SARAH, of Cork, married Burrowes Campbell a barrister at law in December 1794. [WHM.568]

WILLCOCKS, WILLIAM, Mayor of Cork in 1793. [CBC]

WILLIAMS, BARBARA, a widow in Cork, will, 1812. [PWI]

WILLIAMS, SAMUEL, a merchant in Cork, will, 1795. [PWI]

WILLIAMS ROBERT, Customs searcher in Cork, 1666. [CSPI.1666]

WILLIAMSON, Mr, Commander of the Duke of York married Miss Lippits, in Cork during February 1764. [FDJ.3841]

WILLIS, Captain, Commander of the Echo, married Miss Clarke of Cork, there in February 1764. [FDJ.3841]

WILLS, THOMAS, a gentleman in Cork, will, 1741. [PWI]

WILSON, GARTWRIGHT, on behalf of her husband Robert Wilson, in the parish of St Finbarr's, barony of Cork, deposition, 1641. [TCD.825.243]

WILY, THOMAS, in Cork, a letter, 1752. [PRONI.D1044.11]

WINTHROP, BENJAMIN, a merchant in Cork, will, 1730. [PWI]

WINTHROP, WILLIAM, Mayor of Cork in 1744. [CBC]

WITHERAL, JOSEPH, Mayor of Cork in 1760. [CBC]

WITHERS, ELIZABETH, a spinster in Cork, will, 1798. [PWI]

WOLFE, NICHOLAS, a linen draper in Cork, died there in February 1764. [FDJ.3838]

WOODLEY, FRANCIS, in Cork, will, 1798. [PWI]

WOODLEY, JOSEPH, a gentleman, was admitted as a Freeman of Cork in 1792. [CCCA]; will, 1809. [PWI]

WOODLEY, Mrs, wife of Mr Woodley an attorney, died in Cork in 1766. [FDJ.4093]

WOODROFFE, SARAH, a widow in Cork, will, 1740. [PWI]

WOODS, EDMOND, an ironmonger in Cork, will, 103. [PWI]

WOODS, GEORGE, was admitted as a Freeman of Cork in 1741. [CCCA]

WOOD, RUSSELL, a gentleman in Cork, will, 1748. [PWI]

WOODS, Mr, a peruke-maker, and the widow Crofts, were married in Cork in September 1770. [FLJ.74]

WOODWARD, RICHARD, a tallow chandler, was admitted as a Freeman of Cork in 1761. [CCCA]

WOODWARD, RICHARD, a shoemaker, was admitted as a Freeman of Cork in 1784. [CCCA]

WOOLEY, THOMAS, a chandler, was admitted as a Freeman of Cork in 1760. [CCCA]

WOOLFE, ARTHUR, Attorney General, was admitted as a Freeman of Cork in 1790. [CCCA]

WOULFE, ROBERT, a silk mercer in Cork, will, 1757. [PWI]

WOOTH, EDWARD, was admitted as a Freeman of Cork in 1727. [CCCA]

WRENNE.WILLIAM, in Christchurch parish, Cork, in 1659. [C]

WRIGHT, GEORGE, in Christchurch parish, Cork, in 1659. [C]

WRIGHT, JOHN, was admitted as a Freeman of Cork in 1736. [CCCA]

WRIGHT, JOHN, Collector at Baltimore, was admitted as a Freeman of Cork in 1800. [CCCA]

WRIGHT, LOWRY, a merchant in Cork, a covenant with James Hamilton in County Antrim, in 1668. [PRONI.D1071.A.4.2.28]

WRIGHT, WILLIAM, a cooper, was admitted as a Freeman of Cork in 1788. [CCCA]

WRIXON, BENJAMIN, a merchant, was admitted as a Freeman of Cork in 1770. [CCCA]

WRIXON, EDWARD, a gentleman, was admitted as a Freeman of Cork in 1772. [CCCA]

WRIXON, HENRY, was admitted as a Freeman of Cork in 1757. [CCCA]

WRIXON, HENRY, of Barrygiblin, was admitted as a Freeman of Cork in 1763. [CCCA]

WRIXON, JOHN, a gentleman, was admitted as a Freeman of Cork in 1739. [CCCA]

WRIXON, JOHN, a merchant, was admitted as a Freeman of Cork in 1765 [CCCA]

WRIXON, JOHN, Mayor of Cork in 1762. [CBC]

WRIXON, JOHN, a merchant, was admitted as a Freeman of Cork in 1788. [CCCA]

WRIXON, NICHOLAS, a gentleman, was admitted as a Freeman of Cork in 1763. [CCCA]

WRIXON, ROBERT, was admitted as a Freeman of Cork in 1737. [CCCA]; Will dated 1 November 1757, codicil dated 10 November 1757, proved 16 December 1768. Will refers to the family vault at Ballyclough, his brother John, brother Henry, sons John and Benjamin, daughter Bridget. [DRD]

WRIXON, ROBERT, Mayor of Cork in 1750. [CBC]

WRIXON, ROBERT, a gentleman, was admitted as a Freeman of Cork in 1769. [CCCA]

WRIXON, WILLIAM, of Barrygiblin, was admitted as a Freeman of Cork in 1782. [CCCA]

YEAMANS, RICHARD, a gentleman, was admitted as a Freeman of Cork in 1738. [CCCA]

YELVERTON, BARRY, a barrister, was admitted as a Freeman of Cork in 1769. [CCCA]

YORK, WILLIAM, a Judge, was admitted as a Freeman of Cork in 1743. [CCCA]

YOUNG, GEORGE, in Christchurch parish, Cork, in 1659. [C]

YOUNG, Captain JOHN, late of the 52nd Regiment of Foot, died in Cork in 1766. [FDJ.4060]

YOUNG, ROGER, a merchant and silk thrower, was admitted as a Freeman of Cork in 1713. [CCCA]

CPSIA information can be obtained
at www.ICGtesting.com
Printed in the USA
LVOW10s0626150318
569962LV00025B/408/P

9 780806 358468